MODERN GYMNASTICS

Systematic Training for Jumping Horses

JIM WOFFORD

First Published in 2013 by Equine Network

Equine Network/Practical Horseman
2520 55th Street, Suite 210
Boulder, CO 80301
303-625-1600
www.equisearch.com

Edited by Sandra Cooke
Cover and Book Design by Lauryl Suire Eddlemon
Editor: Sandra Oliynyk, *Practical Horseman*
Managing Editor: Stacey Nedrow-Wigmore, *Practical Horseman*
Photographs: Stacey Nedrow-Wigmore
Diagrams: Philip Cooper
Cover, small photo: © Szemere Photography
Back cover, top photo: Mandy Collins

PRACTICAL HORSEMAN
PracticalHorsemanMag.com

Copyright © 2013 Cruz Bay Publishing dba Equine Network

All rights reserved. No part of this publication may be produced or transmitted in any form or by any means, electronically or mechanically, including photocopying, recording, or by any information storage or retrieval system, without prior written permission from the publisher.

Order by calling 800-952-5813 or online at www.HorseBooksEtc.com

The authors and publisher shall have neither liability nor responsibility to any person or entity with respect to any loss or damage caused or alleged to be caused directly or indirectly by the information contained in this book. While the book is as accurate as the authors can make it, there may be errors, omissions or inaccuracies.

Library of Congress Control Number: 2013935262

Printed in USA

Contents

Acknowledgements — *v*

Key to Gymnastic Exercises — *vii*

Introduction — *1*

Chapter 1 The Horse — *3*

Chapter 2 The Rider — *7*

Chapter 3 Training Facilities — *13*

Chapter 4 Beginning Gymnastics — *17*

Chapter 5 Advanced Jumping — *43*

Chapter 6 Cross-Country Gymnastics — *69*

Chapter 7 Exercises for Correcting Errors — *93*

Chapter 8 Conclusion — *107*

Bibliography — *109*

About the Author — *110*

Acknowledgements

Some of my earliest memories on horseback are of jumping down a line of gymnastics and enjoying the sensation. I soon found that gymnastic jumping is a powerful training technique, one that I continue to use half a century after I first learned to jump.

Before I tell you about gymnastic jumping, I will tell you about myself. My family has been involved with horses for nearly 100 years, and that influence on my attitudes towards horses is unmistakable. I grew up in a family where my father, both brothers and one sister-in-law had ridden in the Olympics, and one cousin was a champion steeplechase jockey. Combine such a family background with a young man whose appetite for learning about horses was insatiable, and a book like this was probably inevitable.

While I have been fortunate to study under many talented and knowledgeable horsemen, the two who have had the greatest influence on my thinking are Bertalan de Némethy and Jack Le Goff.

At the same time, no one learns everything they know about horses from one source. I am lucky to have been surrounded throughout my life by horses of all shapes, sizes and abilities, and I have learned something from each one—a process that continues to this day.

I have been surrounded by talented riders and horses in my riding and training careers, and that trend continues in my more recent career as an author. I want to acknowledge their efforts; this is their book, as well as mine. Bill Steinkraus is my lodestar in all things equestrian. You may not feel his gentle touch on this book, but it is there. Sharon Anthony and Kevin Freeman read my manuscript of this book in an early stage, and their suggestions were invaluable. (They now appreciate the meaning of the term "rough draft.") When I accidentally deleted entire chapters of text or committed some other colossal computer error, Merrilyn Saint talked me down off the ledge and restored sanity to my world and the missing text to my computer.

In order to illustrate this book, students and friends gave up days from their lives, brought their horses and waited cheerfully as Mike Mendell set the next gymnastic. Their generosity to me touched my heart and should be acknowledged here. Each of the gymnastics you see illustrated in this book was built and jumped at Beverly Equestrian, Darrin Mollett and Bill Ballhaus' state-of-the-art facility in The Plains, Virginia. This process completely disrupted the farm's normal routine, but Darrin and Bill were unfailingly helpful and welcoming. It was a thrill to see the entire sequence of gymnastics used in its correct order, and it was fascinating to watch the development of each horse and rider as they went through each gymnastic.

Your enjoyment of this book will be enhanced by Stacey Nedrow-Wigmore's sparkling photos, and Phil Cooper's graphic illustration of each gymnastic will accelerate your learning process. An image may be worth a thousand words, but you have to look at a thousand photos and graphics to choose the right one. I owe Stacey and Phil a thousand thanks for their tireless labors.

My only advice to aspiring authors is "get yourself a good editor." Get an editor who firmly believes that the difference between the almost-perfect word and the perfect word is the difference between the lightning bug and the lightning. I am fortunate to have such an editor in Sandra Cooke, who has the priceless gift of enhancing and amplifying, rather than subduing, the author's voice. While the thoughts, training techniques, opinions and errors here are mine, whatever style and grace you find in the text is Sandra's contribution, and I am profoundly grateful for her help.

I mentioned my family in the opening of my acknowledgements, and I would be remiss if I did not point out that my daughters, their spouses and my four grandsons all view with amused tolerance my absent-minded behavior when I am writing. My long-suffering wife, Gail, deserves special thanks for her patience and understanding.

This is my book, but all the people mentioned above had a hand in its development. I hope you enjoy the result of their efforts. More importantly, I hope that your horses come to understand and enjoy their job once you apply the principles and techniques that are presented here.

Key to Gymnastic Diagrams

Trotting or placing pole, or rail on the ground

Hogsback or triple bar (according to relevant text)

An upright (or vertical) element

The distance between elements

An oxer

Direction one way

Low-wide oxer with a diagonal pole placed across. (See page 89 for further explanation.)

Direction both ways

Key to Gymnastic Diagrams

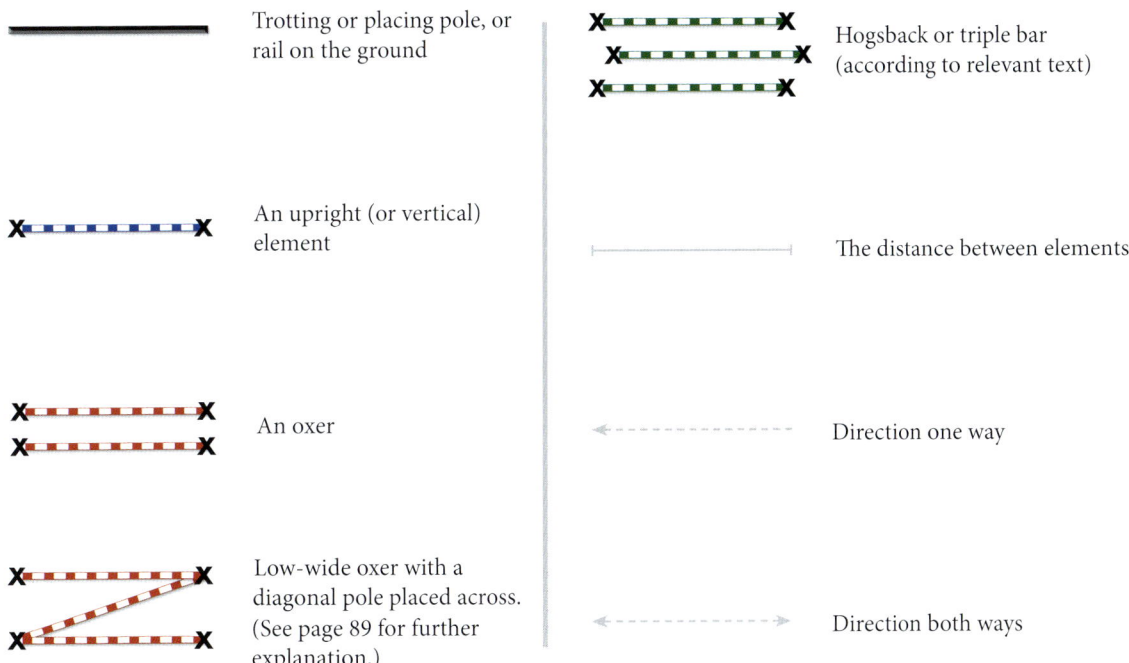

Introduction

Gymnastic jumping is the best tool available to improve your horse's performance. It has existed for nearly 100 years. However, anyone interested in training his or her horse has usually needed to consult a number of books on the subject, picking up a little bit here and a little bit there. Although most of the great riders and trainers I have known over the last 30 years have used these techniques, until now it has been difficult to find a single source book on the topic.

Most of my adult life has been spent teaching horses and riders to jump. Indeed, it has been a rare U.S. team at the Olympics or World Championships that has not had at least one of my students in it. At the 2000 Olympics in Sydney, all four U.S. team members—including David O'Connor, the individual gold medalist—were graduates of my program. In 2004 another of my students, Kim Severson, won the individual silver medal in Athens. Four years later, at the 2008 Beijing Olympics, my former student Gina Miles won another individual silver medal. I hope you will agree that this system of training has withstood the ultimate test … it works in the real world!

You will find in this book a series of gymnastic exercises that will improve the way your horse jumps. These gymnastics are designed to lead you and your horse step-by-step from simple, low exercises for young, inexperienced horses to difficult, complex exercises for talented, experienced horses.

You will also find chapters on selecting a horse (the more suitable your horse, the better your results will be) and the rider's position (there is an inescapable connection between how well you ride and how well your horse goes).

Regardless of your horse's talent and experience, you will find an exercise in this book that will make him a better jumper. At the same time, these exercises are designed to be systematic and progressive. If you practice over some of the easier exercises first, then the more complicated exercises will make more sense to you and your horse when you attempt them.

Every horse is born knowing how to jump. However, when you put the weight of a rider on the horse's back, it will take a lengthy training process before that horse can reach his full potential. A regimen of these gymnastic exercises will improve your and your horse's:

- balance
- technique
- flexibility
- confidence
- fitness

I use the term *gymnastic jumping* to mean placing any two or more obstacles a certain distance apart. This distance will then determine the number and length of your horse's stride or strides between the obstacles. By first repeating and then later varying the gymnastic exercises, your horse's performance will be much improved. The final results will be so rewarding and beneficial that you will be pleased you undertook the process.

You will find this book useful as a tool for either the continued training of your horse or his remedial education. While it can certainly be read cover-to-cover, you can use this book as a reference. Have a rushing problem? Need a new jump layout but not sure what to build or what distances to use between obstacles? Have a horse that runs out? I have some ideas. As you work through my progressive gymnastics, you'll find solutions for these and other training challenges.

However you decide to use it, I am sure you will find something in this book that will improve your horse, which is the true horseman's highest goal.

1
The Horse

If you are going to jump your horse, you might as well have one with the right talent and physique. I prefer horses between 15.3 and 16.1 hands high. Obviously there have been successful horses of every size and shape, but in my opinion, horses within this range tend to be the most balanced and athletic, and certainly balance and athleticism are key ingredients in the making of a good jumper.

It is not theoretically correct, but when evaluating a horse, the first thing I do is "look him in the eye." My ideal horse is the horse I fall in love with again every morning when I see his face hanging over the stable door, looking for breakfast. If you do not like a horse the first time you see him, do not talk yourself into buying him. You will always be secretly unhappy with him, and you won't make the necessary excuses for his inevitable mistakes during the training process.

I prefer horses that are slightly higher at the withers than the croup. In general, the lower a horse is in front, the more skill you will need to present him in balance to an obstacle. If you plan to participate in activities in which speed plays a part (such as hunting, point-to-pointing or eventing), you will want a horse that tends to keep his own balance.

Working from the ground up, the horse should have four normal, well-shaped feet, at least of a size in proportion to his overall body weight. The forelegs should form two parallel lines when viewed from the front. The hind legs should form a vertical line from the point of the hock to the ground. If the hind legs do not form this straight line, they should be set slightly *under* the body, rather than out behind. There are certain conformation flaws that I can accept in a prospective purchase. If the horse is slightly "over" at the knee, it is often a sign that he will snap his knees in the air over a fence. But a horse that is "behind" in his knees is so prone to injury that I will pass him by.

If a horse is cow-hocked or sickle-hocked, I think this concentrates his power under the body. But if his hocks are set wide or—even worse—set wide and behind the body, don't buy him. You will never get him to engage, and he will always run on his forehand.

When you buy a horse, buy one that is not only a good jumper, but one that suits you as well. Make sure to take into account the horse's temperament and its suitability for you. If you weigh 200 pounds and are ham-fisted, do not buy a sensitive 15.3-hand chestnut Thoroughbred mare. If you are a bit timid, you will need a horse that does not take a lot of kicking to get to the other side.

It goes without saying that when choosing a prospect, the quality of all three paces is important. However, if you are selecting the horse for show jumping only, pay the most attention to the canter, which should be smooth and balanced.

In the meantime, you can give the show jumper's walk and trot less attention and emphasis. Some roundness in the show jumper's action is desirable, because it helps to produce a round shape over the jump. On the other hand, horses that are being evaluated for eventing or foxhunting should be correct in all three paces. While racehorses need only to gallop, it is no secret that correct biomechanics lead to soundness, balance and long-term usefulness. Usually, the better the walk, the better the gallop, as they are both four-beat gaits. Watch the horse walk at liberty, and you will get a better idea of his potential to gallop and jump.

If you are going to purchase a prospect that has never been taught to jump, find a horse of the type that I have described above. If it has a lovely, flowing four-beat walk that is straight, smooth and energetic, then you have probably found a horse that will be able to gallop and jump. The most consistent anatomical indicator of jumping ability I have ever found is prominent withers. A horse with prominent withers, built slightly uphill, and with "the look of eagles" is a good prospect.

It is obvious that the horse must be able to see an obstacle in order to jump it, yet people forget to take this into account. During the pre-purchase examination, make sure that your veterinarian pays particular attention to the horse's vision. In addition, while you are training your horse, it is important that you understand how a horse looks at an obstacle.

The horse has *monocular* vision. This means he sees with a fixed field of focus that is approximately 10 degrees in front of the plane of his nose. In other words, for the horse to see obstacles farther ahead in his path he must lift his head and neck and point his nose farther along the line of this approach.

This fact immediately tells us that all of our efforts to bring a horse "round" to the jump are wrong, if by "round" we emphasize only the flexion of the horse at the poll and ignore the engagement of the hindquarters. Allow your horse to approach the obstacle with a comfortable outline and direct your efforts towards approaching the obstacle with him "on contact," not "on the bit." As long as your horse carries his poll higher than his withers, he has enough balance and engagement to jump up to 4 feet (1.2m).

How a Horse Jumps

If you are going to teach your horse to jump, it is important that you know how horses jump. Whether from the trot or the canter, your horse begins his jumping motion with his forehand. He will lower his head and neck slightly, plant both front feet, and then bring his head and neck back and up to begin his jumping motion. As his forehand leaves the ground, his hindquarters will reach forward under his body and propel him along the arc that his forehand has started to produce.

In theory, the horse should describe a perfect half-circle in the air with his body. This arc is referred to somewhat inaccurately as the *bascule*, a French term from the verb meaning "to rock or swing." The takeoff point will largely govern the shape of the bascule. In theory, the horse's take off should be the height of the fence away from the fence. For example, the horse should take off 3 feet away from a 3-foot fence. He should reach the high point of his bascule over the highest point of the fence, and land the height of the fence beyond the fence. Once we know the shape of the perfect jump, we can start to analyze the flaws in our horse's jumping technique as we go through our training program.

However, we should not be blinded by theory. Over small obstacles in the real world, both the takeoff and the landing points are farther away from the obstacle than the height of that obstacle.

Use your knowledge of theory to measure your horse's performance. For example, his jump will be what we call "flat" if the approach speed has been too great for the size and shape of the jump, or if the takeoff point has been too far away from the first rail. If the arc of the jump begins too close to the obstacle, forming a square outline, we call it "sticky," "chipping in" or sometimes "putting in a short one." This shape is more often caused by your horse getting behind your leg at the point of takeoff, rather than taking off too close to the jump.

Once you have analyzed the shape of your horse's arc and compared it in your mind with the perfect arc that you are trying to produce, the corrections that you should make become more obvious. For example, if he is jumping too flat, slow him down. If he is sticky over his obstacles, bring him to the fence with a more forward rhythm and close your legs more strongly at the point of takeoff. These habits are easier to correct by using a series of gymnastic obstacles than by working over individual obstacles, because you know the number of strides before the next obstacle and, thus, the takeoff point when you arrive at the obstacle. If you have limited experience jumping, be sure to have someone more knowledgeable watching. It can be difficult to analyze your horse's performance while you are also concentrating on not falling off.

The horse's jump can be divided into five phases. They are:

- approach
- takeoff
- flight
- landing
- departure

If your horse's shape in the air over the obstacle is incorrect, it is usually because something has gone wrong either in the approach or the takeoff. Occasionally during gymnastic jumping, the second obstacle of a series will cause problems because, for example, the rider has toppled back in the air over the first obstacle or has fallen forward against the horse's neck during the landing and departure. Remember that the departure from the first obstacle in a line of gymnastic obstacles is the approach to the next. By definition, gymnastic jumps are set in relation to one another.

While dressage as such lies outside the scope of this book, I should point out that the improvement of your horse's performance over obstacles is going to be directly related to the quality of his dressage training. The calmness, balance, engagement and strength that he will gain by a concerted effort to improve his dressage work will directly affect his performance over obstacles. Each time you get a new horse to work with, you must place as much emphasis on his training on the flat as you do on his work over fences.

2
The Rider

The best way to improve your horse's jumping is to improve your own position. In order to find the correct jumping position, you need to adjust your stirrup leathers correctly. To do this, sit in the saddle at the halt and take both feet out of the stirrups. Then let your legs hang straight down, and adjust the stirrup leather until the tread of the stirrup touches the inside of your leg at, or just above, your ankle bone.

Place both feet in the stirrups with the ball of your foot on the tread of the stirrup. Press enough weight into your ankles so that your heels are significantly lower than your toes. The sensation you should have is that the weight moves from the inside of your leg into your heel. When you are seated in the saddle, an onlooker should see about a 90-degree angle behind your knee after you have adjusted your stirrups.

Viewed from the front, your feet should form a slight angle away from the line of the horse's body. This angle varies from rider to rider. In general, it should approximate the angle at which your feet turn when you walk. For example, if you toe out slightly at the walk, your feet should turn away from the horse to about the same degree. If you are pigeon-toed at the walk, your feet will stay more nearly parallel to the horse's body. However, at no time should you attempt to force your lower leg into a position that is not comfortable for your joints. For your purposes, natural and supple should be synonymous.

I will occasionally refer to a "two-point" position, or a "light three-point," so I need to explain my terminology.

For example, when I mention a two-point position, I am referring to the two points of contact between your knees and the saddle. While you are in the two-point position, your knees and ankles should support your weight, and your buttocks should not touch the saddle. The grip point is more towards the back of the knee than towards the kneecap.

This is the position you should use when:

- galloping

- jumping

- posting (rising) to the trot

- you want to take your weight off your horse's back.

Because of the importance of your two-point position, I am going to give you a couple of exercises to strengthen and improve it.

The first exercise is to **post without stirrups**. This is an excellent method to develop and strengthen the muscles you will need to gallop and jump. If you can rise at the trot without stirrups for five minutes, you are probably fit enough for competitive activities.

The second exercise is to **keep your stirrups, assume the two-point position and stay suspended over your horse's back at the trot and the canter**. Press your weight down into your ankles and practice absorbing the shock of your horse's movement with your knees instead of your hips. Keep your stirrup leathers vertical throughout this exercise, your hands off your horse's neck, your back slightly arched and your head and eyes forward. This exercise will help you improve your jumping position.

Another position I will refer to is the "light three-point." While maintaining the two points of contact behind your knees, close your knee angle and allow your weight to settle back into the saddle—**but keep your shoulders in front of your hips**. Three points now support the weight of your body: your two seat bones and your pubic bone. I suggest that you use a light three-point position in the approach to obstacles.

In a "full three-point," your shoulders would be over your hips, your stirrup leathers would be longer and you would be in a dressage position. Although you cannot improve your horse's jumping without improving his dressage, that topic is outside the focus of this book.

When you are either in a two-point or a light three-point position, the grip of your lower leg against the saddle should feel evenly distributed between the inside of your knee and the inside of your ankle. This grip can move up and down your leg as the situation dictates. If your horse tends to be sluggish in front of an obstacle, your grip must move lower in your leg towards the heel in order to urge him forward. If your horse "cracks his back" over an obstacle or bucks on landing, your inside knee grip should be very strong.

If you make a mistake when jumping, you should emphasize the grip of your knee rather than the grip of your heel. Although gripping with the knee may cause your lower leg to swing, at least it will help you stay attached to your horse—and if you are attached to your horse, you can improve. If you grip with your heels, however, your knees will come away from the saddle and you will have the sensation of riding a greased pig. This is upsetting to your horse and can spoil both his landing and his departure from the obstacle, quickly leading to a downward learning curve.

Because you will often need to rise out of the saddle when riding, the inner surface of your thigh should not actually grip the saddle. However, the muscles on the *outside* of your thigh are very helpful in attaching you to the saddle and, therefore, to your horse.

Working our way up in your position, we arrive next at the hip and the small of the back. There should be a slight forward angle at your hip when you are seated with jumping-length stirrups. The small of your back should show a slight forward arch at your waist, your back should be flat, shoulders square, head erect and your eyes looking straight ahead through your horse's ears.

Once your upper body is in the correct position, adjust the reins so that the inside point of your elbow is just in front of the point of your hip. Then form a straight line from your elbow to your hand, and through the reins to the horse's mouth.

Hold your reins as if you were carrying a plate of soup: Your thumbs are on top of the reins and your hands remain the width of your horse's mouth apart. Maintain this relationship when riding both on a straight line and through turns or circles.

When your horse jumps, maintain the straight line from your elbow to his mouth. Notice that the more your horse bascules over a fence, the lower his mouth goes in relation to his withers—and therefore the lower down the neck your hand must travel in order to retain this classical straight line.

When we speak of a rider who has "good hands" over jumps, we actually mean that the rider has supple elbows and poised shoulders. The sensation you should have during the bascule is that you have an elastic band tied to the back of your elbow, and your horse stretches this elastic forward and down. Take care not to suddenly increase or decrease this elastic contact. Because the stability and sensitivity of your hands are based on the security of your position, you must continually improve your lower-leg position.

Vision

When I first learned how to jump, I was taught to look above the obstacle. I no longer agree with this technique. There are not many sports where the coach tells the athlete to look away from what they are doing. In the approach to an obstacle, I want you to keep your eyes focused on the top rail until it disappears between your horse's ears. The reason for this is that you will be able to predict your stride in front of the obstacle more accurately if you see the obstacle. This process is known as "timing." **Timing is the rider's ability to predict and influence the remaining increments of a stride in front of the obstacle.** Your timing will improve immediately if you watch the obstacle in the approach.

Look at the front rail of your oxers, look at the top rail of verticals and look at the back rail of triple bars.

Watching the obstacle may not produce instant accuracy, but it will produce instant harmony between you and your horse. Timing is a skill, one that takes time to develop. Meanwhile, worry less about *where* you are going to take off in front of the jump, and concentrate more on *how* you are going to take off. By this I mean that riding to the jump in a steady rhythm is far more important than "seeing your distance."

Equipment

Just as you should never jump without someone else in the area, you should never jump without a helmet. That helmet should fit correctly and must have a harness strap that keeps it in place during a fall. If you are going to be jumping at speeds faster than a show-ring canter, consider using the modern protective jackets and air vests that are now available.

When training your horse in gymnastic jumping, use the mildest equipment possible. A plain hollow-mouth or flat-ring snaffle and simple noseband should suffice. It may be that you have to use a stronger bit when at a competition, but try to use simple equipment at home as much as possible, and train your horse calmly and classically. This will give you the best possible chance to make lasting improvements in his performance.

Saddles

First of all, the saddle should fit your horse. Next, it should be suitable for jumping and comfortable for you. Find the low point of the saddle while mounted at the halt. Move back and forth along the gullet until you find the low point of the seat. Then adjust your stirrup leathers as described at the beginning of this chapter. If the saddle fits you correctly, you should then find that your knees fit just behind the knee roll. I do not like saddles with a pronounced knee roll, as I find that they cause most riders' lower legs to swing backwards. The new close-contact saddles seem to be the best for all-around jumping.

Protective Boots

Your horse should wear protective boots of some kind on all four legs. I prefer leather boots with a foam lining and strap and buckle closings. While boots with hook-and-loop closings such as Velcro® are sufficient for everyday use, they tend to come undone in competition.

Full leather boots afford the best protection for eventers, racehorses, young horses and field hunters with less-than-good action, while show hunters and jumpers should use open-fronted boots. If your horse has any tendency at all to overreach, he should always wear bell (overreach) boots on his front feet when jumping.

Effects of Gymnastic Jumping on the Rider's Position

Gymnastic jumping will have an extremely beneficial effect on your position. There are several reasons for this:

- The predictability of the striding allows you to be prepared for the horse's jumping motion.

- You will be able to repeat the same exercise, making adjustments in your lower leg, upper body and so on, in order to find the exact balance point over your horse at any time throughout the jumping effort.

- Gymnastic jumping will also improve your timing. Look at the next obstacle when landing over the preceding obstacle. Because you have measured the distance between elements carefully, you know the desired outcome. Use this knowledge to predict the number of remaining strides. Tell yourself that you are a certain number of strides away from the next obstacle and then ride to that obstacle in the correct rhythm and on the correct number of strides. This will help develop your "eye for distance."

Gymnastic 5 on page 34, which introduces your horse to the concept of a "bounce," is of special value when you are working on your own position.

⬆ You are not always going to have as large a jump crew as shown here, but even if it is only you and a friend, develop a meticulous attitude towards building your gymnastics. Use a tape measure when you set your jumps. There are enough variables in the training of horses already. Make sure you do not introduce another variable by building gymnastics with a different distance than you had intended. Measure the inside distance from the back of the last standard to the front of the next standard to make sure you are going to use the distance you had meant to use. If you are working in an enclosed ring or an indoor arena, also measure from the side of the first standard to the wall. As you build the rest of your gymnastic line, measure from the side of the next standards to the wall. Do this with all the standards so that your gymnastic line is parallel to the wall or arena fence. I have found that when the gymnastic line is not parallel to the wall, it can cause your horse to "drift" as he jumps the line of obstacles. You will find that the disciplined attitude you have towards building your gymnastics will lead to a more disciplined attitude when it comes time to jump the gymnastics. This in turn will help your entire attitude towards the training of your horse become more disciplined and organized, which will lead to a well-trained horse. And a well-trained horse is the best friend a horseman can have.

3
Training Facilities

If you are going to train your horse to jump, you need a training area. The most important requisite of a jumping arena is good footing. ***There must be some displacement of the footing in order to absorb the concussion of jumping.*** The surface does not have to be of any particular material, but your horse should be able to make a hoofprint in the surface when moving normally around the arena. In order to determine this, walk out onto the surface of your training area and dig your heel into the surface slightly. You should be able to make a print in the surface. Another good rule of thumb is that after your horse goes by, an onlooker should be able to see an outline of his foot in the surface.

Landing areas should be suitable for jumping onto because repetition is part of learning. We want to repeat the effort where the footing is not going to give your horse a bad experience, especially when jumping down—for example, off banks. The repetitive nature of training horses to jump means a lot of wear and tear on the footing of the takeoff and landing sites. This is especially true when jumping on wet ground. Be sure to repair the damage to the footing to ensure the best possible training conditions for your horse. Likewise, if the ground is hard, add shavings or some form of sand to the landing in order to maintain your horse's soundness and confidence.

It is of definite benefit to have your jumping area enclosed by a fence or a wall of some type. This will help your horse concentrate better and is invaluable if you should happen to become disconnected from him for whatever reason while training. If your arena is outdoors, make sure that the drainage is good enough for it to be usable in all but the most inclement weather conditions.

Safety should never be far from your mind; you must have a ground person present at all times when you are jumping. In addition, a person on the ground, especially one who can make knowledgeable observations about your and your horse's performance, is of great value. Besides the safety aspect, the ground person's role is to set the jumps, to add obstacles as the training grid progresses in difficulty and to adjust the heights and spreads according to the horse's reaction. The ground person should be able to move obstacles, reset poles and generally make himself useful. It is extremely difficult to do any kind of gymnastic jumping if you have to dismount and reset obstacles yourself while trying to train your horse.

General Comments Regarding the Gymnastics

As you progress through the training exercises described in this book, keep these simple, yet important, guidelines in mind.

First, never worry that you have set the heights too low, especially early in the training session and most especially when schooling young or inexperienced horses. It is easy to raise the heights and increase the spreads later on as your horse gains confidence and experience, whereas his confidence is very difficult to re-establish if he has lost it early in the session.

As the exercises in this book become more technical, make sure to lower the height of the preceding jumps when you add the next obstacle in a progression. Once you explain the new exercise to your horse with the obstacles set low, he will not be as bothered by height and spread when the time comes to increase them. Always finish your training session on a good note.

I have developed these exercises over 30 years of doing clinics, and they have been jumped safely by thousands of horses. Remember, however, that they were used in clinic and group-lesson situations. Every horse is different; use your common sense in adjusting the distances. If your horse takes an average stride and reacts in a normal fashion in jumping situations, these distances should be comfortable for him. If he has an unusually long or short stride, on the other hand, by all means adjust the distances to suit him.

Measuring Distances

When setting distances, be very precise about the measurement between obstacles or between cavalletti and obstacles. When I use the term "cavalletti," I mean poles laid on the ground at *measured* intervals. There are already enough variables involved in the training of horses. Do not introduce more variables by being inaccurate with the measurement between obstacles that you set up.

Use a measuring tape to set the exercises; then practice pacing the distance between the obstacles. This will accomplish two things:

- You will know that you are jumping an exercise that is set and measured correctly.

- Your step will become more accurate, which is a nice skill to have when you pace a combination at a competition.

I am obsessive about setting up exercises symmetrically in the arena. When jumping more than one obstacle in a row, make the center of the exercise parallel to the long side of the arena. You can do this by measuring from the first standard of your exercise to one wall and then from the last standard of the exercise to the same wall, making sure that you get the same distance both at the beginning and the end of the line.

Why take this trouble? Because if the distance is inconsistent and the line is skewed, you may teach your horse to jump more in one direction than another.

I like to see symmetrical cups, too, with all the pins facing the same way. In addition, a little time and effort taken in raking the footing will go a long way towards maintaining the base of your arena's footing, and maintaining your horse's soundness and enthusiasm for jumping.

I have used feet as a unit of measurement throughout this book. I understand that this is not terribly modern, but it is the way I was trained and I think in those units. However, for the convenience of those more modern, you will find metric measurements in parentheses beside mine.

A word on how to measure: When measuring between cavalletti, I measure the inside distance from one pole to another. When I measure canter cavalletti, I do the same. When placing jumps in sequence, I measure from the back rail of the last element to the first rail of the succeeding element. Remember to change the distance between elements when you change the spread of one of the oxers in an exercise.

I have assumed that all of your rails are 12 feet (3.6m) long. If this is not the case, remember to adjust the relationships when measuring distances between angled rails.

To ensure the safest possible experience for yourself and your horse, follow these basic guidelines:

- Always wear a helmet with the chinstrap fastened.

- Do not jump alone.

- Do not jump on hard ground.

- Place your ground lines at least in the vertical plane of the front element—never behind it. (Ground lines are not entirely necessary; indeed, you can do away with them once your horse gains some confidence in his jumping.)

- The ends of each rail resting in the jump cup should be at least one inch from the standard. Do not "wedge" the standards. If your horse makes a mistake, the rail should come out of the cups.

- Always remove all cups from the standards when they are not in use. Your horse may cut himself on an open cup left on a standard if he swerves or "drifts" down a series of obstacles.

When adding elements, the variation of the height and spread of the obstacles is more important than the actual measurement. For example, verticals will look higher to your horse in a line of fences if the oxers are lower and wider.

A 12-inch (30cm) variation from one obstacle to another is entirely acceptable and will cause your horse to concentrate and make a more accurate assessment of the situation.

Oxers will not have the required effect on your horse's bascule until they are at least as wide as they are high. Whenever schooling a young horse, set the initial heights low. Then introduce him to changes in height and spread by small, that is 3-inch (7.5cm), graduated changes. Later on, more experienced horses should confront situations in which the first obstacle in the line is the highest and also situations in which there is an extreme variation in height and spread from one obstacle to another. You will make more progress if you jump your horse more times over lower obstacles than you will by attempting to jump fewer, larger obstacles in the training session.

4
Beginning Gymnastics

This chapter addresses the horse that has some jumping experience but has not been introduced to more technical aspects of the sport. Never forget that it is essential to maintain the calmness and confidence of your horse throughout his training over obstacles. If you preserve these two elements, you will be able to make the most rapid progress with him and produce the most long-lasting and beneficial effects.

Approach these exercises at a calm, regular, balanced pace with quite a long or possibly even loose contact. I place a great deal of emphasis on awakening the horse's initiative at an early stage of training and attempting to maintain that initiative throughout his career; thus, my emphasis on soft reins.

Do not ride your horse as if you must give him a "good" ride, but rather attempt to be an intelligent passenger. Once he gets to the obstacle, he must arrange his footwork and propel his body over the fence. At this point it is your job to stay out of his way. If you run into difficulties, you should either lower the obstacle or, if you are jumping gymnastic obstacles in sequence, remove the last obstacle and lower the others until you get your horse going forward again. Once he is calm and balanced, you can resume the exercise.

Your goals are for your horse to maintain his rhythm, balance and regularity of stride over obstacles. I think that we should teach your horse to balance himself, not to expect us to balance him. An excellent exercise is to count in rhythm with his stride as he proceeds down the line of obstacles. For example, if you have obstacles set up to produce one stride in between them, then as the horse lands over the first element you should be able to say out loud "land." Then as he reaches the end of his stride before leaving the ground over the second obstacle you should be able to say "one" in rhythm with the takeoff. If there are succeeding obstacles, you should be able to repeat this down the entire gymnastic line.

This sounds like a very simple exercise, but you will find it surprisingly difficult to perform correctly while your horse is jumping. You may find that the timing of your voice is not in rhythm with your horse's landing; this is the most common mistake that I see in my clinics when students attempt this exercise. Riders who make this mistake usually have some weakness in their jumping position that causes a loss of balance. This loss of balance is very distracting, because the rider will think more about self-preservation than about maintaining balance and rhythm in the landing phase of the jump. If you land out of balance, it means there is something wrong with your position. If there is something wrong with your position, it is usually that your lower-leg position is faulty. Most of the time, if you improve your lower-leg position, you will improve your landing after jumps.

Your horse should maintain an absolutely steady, regular cadence down the line of obstacles. Your counting should also be steady, regular and cadenced. Riders who become agitated when jumping will find that their voices rise in volume and pitch. Many riders will quicken the cadence of their counting until their voices and their horses' strides are no longer in synchrony. Many times, these are the same riders who will blame their horses for rushing.

You can do Gymnastic 1 in either a jumping or a dressage saddle. If you ride in a dressage saddle, shorten your stirrups one hole, because the added height of your horse's step over the poles will cause you to need a bit more stability than if you were riding on the flat. For the rest of the exercises you will need a jumping saddle.

Practice keeping your eye on the next object in your horse's path. For example, if you are trotting towards a pole on the ground, look through his ears at the pole until it goes out of sight. With young horses and inexperienced riders, I do not ask the rider to alter the horse's step in front of the pole because I want to awaken the horse's initiative. Whether he takes a slightly long step or adds an additional step before the pole, I am equally satisfied. If he steps on the pole, the chances are good that he will learn from the experience and not do it again. If he continues to step on the poles on the ground, I suggest that the rider find another prospect, as this one is probably too dumb to improve over obstacles.

Look sequentially at each object in your horse's path, even when there are additional objects. If you are trotting over a series of ground poles followed by an obstacle, look at the first pole, and then keep your eye on the obstacle until

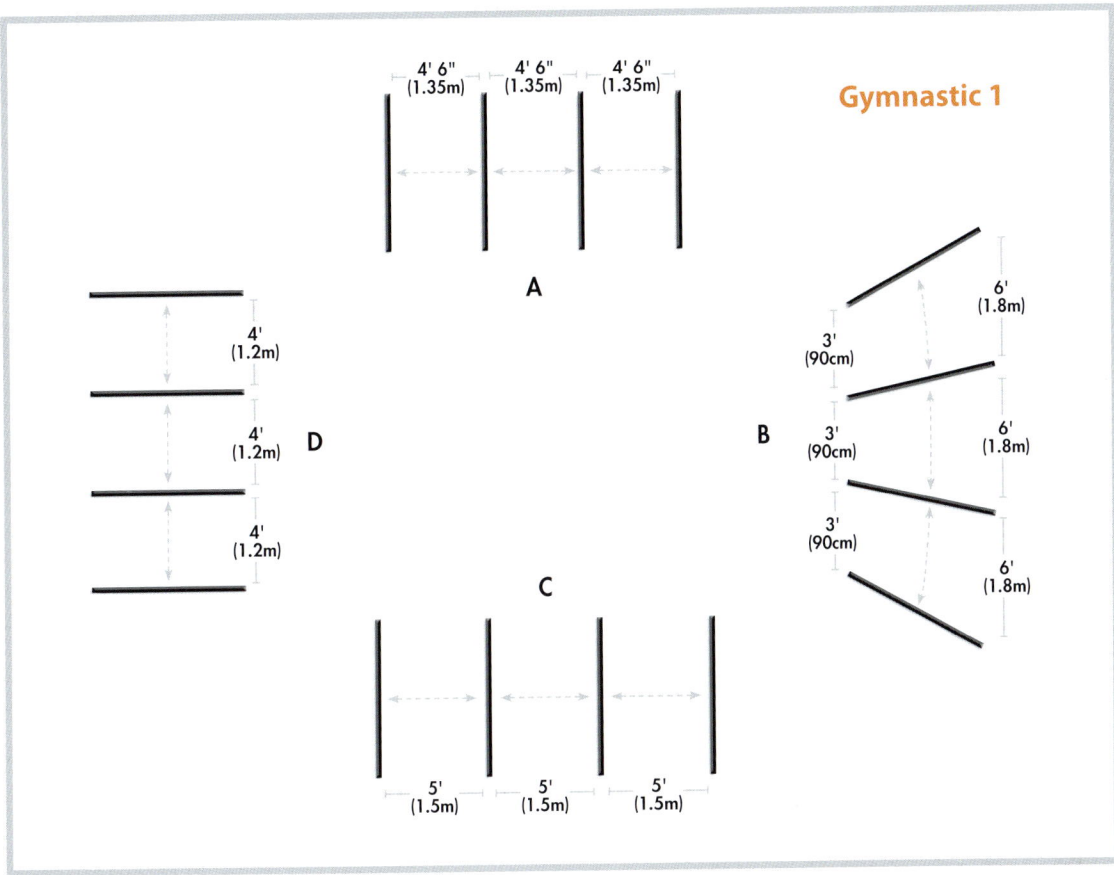

it goes out of sight between your horse's ears. (The ground poles are so close together it is difficult to follow them with your eye.) This will help you maintain a straight line through the gymnastic exercises and will also help you develop your timing. You can't see your stride if you don't see the jump.

These exercises rely on cavalletti to stabilize your horse's length of step, speed and balance. If an obstacle follows the cavalletti, use the posting (rising) trot until your horse steps over the last pole; then softly lower your seat to the saddle. This will ensure that you are in touch with your horse's back when he leaves the ground.

Do not lean forward while negotiating the cavalletti. When your horse leaves the ground to jump the obstacle, you should have the sensation that he has brought his withers up towards your chest.

For all cavalletti work, and indeed all sorts of jumping work, your horse should wear protective boots or bandages on his legs as, especially when stepping over poles, he may knock his legs while learning to coordinate them.

Gymnastic 1 (above)

Gymnastic 1 is designed to introduce your horse to stepping over poles on the ground in an organized manner. Dressage horses can also benefit

⬆ GYMNASTIC 1A If your horse is going to jump, he needs to work over cavalletti (usually four poles on the ground at pre-determined distances). Allison Springer and Sophia show you the benefits of cavalletti work. Sophia's hocks and stifles are active, and her forehand is light and supple. When you work over cavalletti, I want you to copy Allison's position. Her stirrups are adjusted correctly, producing a 90-degree angle behind her knee when she is seated. Her back is slightly arched at the waist, her shoulder is slightly in front of her hip, she is looking forward through Sophia's ears and she has a straight line from her elbow to her horse's mouth.

These cavalletti (shown as A in the graphic on page 19) are set at a distance of 4-foot-6 between each pole, which will produce a rhythmical working trot for horses of normal size.

from this first gymnastic, because no jumping is involved. Your emphasis here should be on the rhythm of your horse's trot, and the calmness and regularity of his step as he negotiates the cavalletti. Your horse should step over the ground poles with relaxed back muscles, and his head and neck should lower slightly, in order for him to measure his step to the next pole.

The four exercises that comprise Gymnastic 1 will fit comfortably in a 75 x 150-foot (22.8m x 45.7m) arena.

After you have warmed your horse up at the walk, trot and canter, then trot into the exercise marked **A** in the diagram on page 19. Cavalletti set at this distance will produce a working trot for most horses. These exercises are all designed for horses with some jumping experience. If your

GYMNASTIC 1B In addition to work in straight lines, cavalletti can be used to teach your horse lateral flexibility. Allison and Sophia are a good illustration of lateral bending to the left. They are working over the cavalletti shown as **B** in the graphic on page 19. Allison has chosen her path through the curved cavalletti carefully, and that path is comfortable for Sophia's length of step. You can use these cavalletti to play with the length of your horse's step while you trot through them. It is interesting to note that if we erased the cavalletti in this image, Allison and Sophia would appear to be trotting on a 20-meter circle with very correct mechanics.

GYMNASTIC 1C Use the cavalletti to determine the length of your horse's step. Later in your training, this flexibility will transfer to your horse's canter stride. Darrin Mollett and Beverly's Gamble are working through cavalletti set at 5 feet, shown as **C** on the graphic on page 19. While this is only a 6-inch difference from the first cavalletti (shown as **A** on page 19), you can see the effect of the longer distance between the poles on "Gambler's" step. Darrin's correct mechanics contribute to her horse's performance. It is amazing how well your horse goes, when you ride well.

horse is extremely green, he probably should not be attempting this exercise yet. However, if he is slightly inexperienced or is an experienced jumper but has not done much work over cavalletti, you can pull the first and third poles in towards the centerline of the arena. This will produce a 9-foot (2.7m) distance between two poles. Horses find this exercise easier and will soon become stable and regular at the trot, which is always your goal. You can then put the four poles together as shown in the diagram and work in both directions over four of them on the ground. After you have established your horse's balance and rhythm here, you can proceed to the curved poles in Gymnastic 1B.

At the posting trot, proceed on a circle in either direction through **B**. Keep your horse's direction adjusted so that the length of his step on the curve feels the same as it did over **A**.

Once you and your horse have become adept at this, you can then start to enter, for example, closer to the 3-foot (90cm) end of the poles where the distance is shorter, and then let your horse angle away from the center of the circle. This will cause him to go from a working trot to a medium trot or possibly, if your angle becomes too great, even take a couple of steps of extended trot. If your horse takes two steps between the poles or breaks into a canter, you have probably asked too much flexibility from him. Aim closer to the 3-foot (90cm) end of the curve, and enter **B** again at the posting trot.

Alternatively, you can enter from the outside of **B**, where the rails are farther apart. This will cause your horse to take quite a large step at first. Guide him towards the 3-foot (90cm) distance between the last two poles. This will bring him back to a working, or even a slightly collected, trot. Having worked in both directions over **B**, including being able to angle both ways, you can then proceed to Gymnastic 1C.

The poles positioned at **C** will produce the sensation of an extended trot and you may find that your horse cannot reach enough in his fourth step to get out over the last pole without "chipping in" an additional step. Simply remove the last pole and continue. You will find that, after a couple of days' work over cavalletti, your horse gets the message and you can replace the fourth pole. You should work in both directions over the 5-foot (1.5m) poles at **C** until your horse can maintain his regularity and length of step. After a short break, proceed to Gymnastic 1D.

These four rails on the ground, set 4 feet (1.2m) apart, will produce a collected trot.

Although this exercise can be ridden either posting or sitting, you should definitely use a rising trot until your horse becomes adjusted to them. Using rising, rather than sitting, trot encourages your horse to lift his back while he elevates his step. In addition, it will be less complicated and will allow you to work on his cadence, rather than worrying about your position. Again, work both ways through **D** until your horse is relaxed and steady in his balance and rhythm. He should be able to deal with the rails without any interruption in the flow of his movement, changing only the length of his step to adapt to the various distances that you have put in his path.

After another break, you can now link these four elements together in order to produce various transitions that will be of great benefit in teaching your horse to be flexible. For example, enter **A** on the right hand in a working trot, where the rails are 4-foot-6 (1.35m) apart. As you leave **A,** turn right in such a fashion that you produce an arc through **B** that causes your horse to change the length of his step from working to collected trot. In other words, start **B** from the outside in. This will put your horse into a slightly collected frame. Proceed directly then to **C**, which will produce an extended trot. After the extended trot at **C**, turn right and enter the shorter cavalletti at **D**.

If your horse has difficulty with this, you can do **A, B** and **C** as I have described and then, in a posting trot, circle (or repeat a circle until your horse has settled down to a working trot), turn and enter **D**, thus producing a collected trot. If you have successfully done this, walk, reward your horse and let him relax and consider his effort while you plan your next series of repetitions through these exercises. When you resume the posting trot, work in both directions and vary the relationship between the exercises to improve and confirm your horse's flexibility.

Take a moment to remind yourself of your horse's bad habits. If he tends to rush at the trot, he will not need too many applications of **C**. He should come from outside in rather from inside out at **B**, as this will cause him to continually rebalance and collect his step rather than rushing forward. If, on the other hand, your horse is choppy-strided or lazy, a bit more emphasis on and a few more repetitions at **B**, going from inside out, will teach him to lengthen his step. The total amount of exercise over these rails in any one period should not exceed 45 minutes, including the periods of rest between exercises.

Gymnastic 2 (below)

This gymnastic is usually your horse's first introduction to gymnastic jumping; make sure he enjoys this work and is relaxed about the exercises. If he displays any tension, you should work through it using this gymnastic, before you proceed to the increasingly difficult gymnastics you will encounter later in this book.

Start with four rails on the ground set 4-foot-6 (1.35m) apart and one more rail 9 feet (2.7m) away, which will form the **A** component. To begin, you should have five poles lying parallel on the ground, with the distances between the

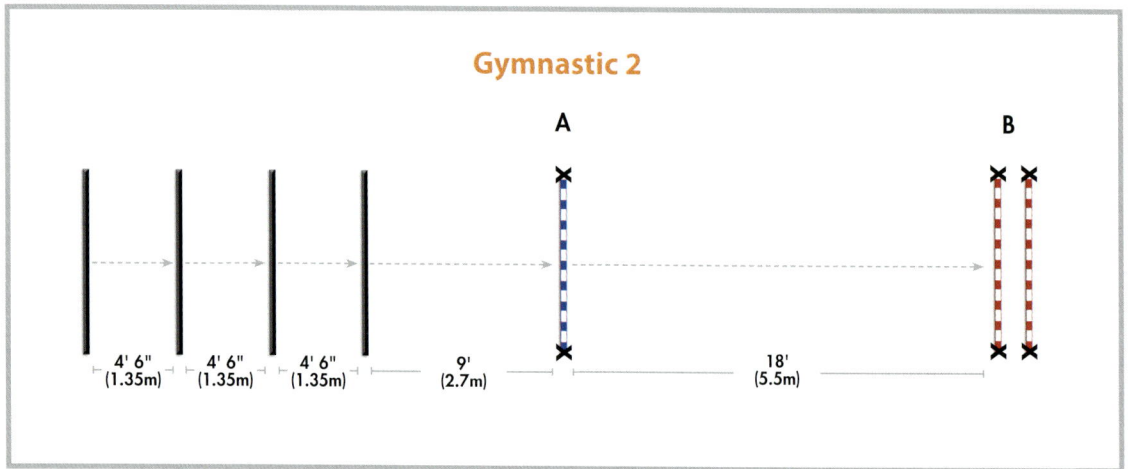

GYMNASTIC 2 is the simplest form of gymnastic. The lovely photo composite you see here shows its complete, final version. What the photo does not show is the gymnastic's careful, progressive development, which starts with five ground poles and gradually increases in difficulty. You must be willing to repeat any part of this gymnastic several times, until you are sure your horse understands the question and calmly provides the answer. Do not build the next element of any gymnastic until your horse is quiet and balanced over the previous element.

In the middle of the cavalletti (four ground poles 4-foot-6 apart), Allison Springer and Sophia are all business. Allison is in the seated phase of her posting trot and displays a 90-degree angle behind her knee. This tells us her stirrup leathers are adjusted correctly. She has a straight line from her elbow to the bit, and her eyes are focused on the vertical. Sophia is calm but attentive and obviously ready for the obstacle.

Rather than leaning over the withers on take-off over the vertical, Allison has allowed Sophia's withers to come up. Her elbows have closed to retain the connection, and the overall impression is of economy of motion.

During the canter stride between the vertical and the oxer, I would like to see Allison completely seated in the approach; however, the feel of the photo is so poised and confident that it is hard to be critical. Allison's stirrup leathers are vertical, her back is slightly arched, she has a straight line from her elbow to Sophia's mouth and her eyes are measuring her distance to the front rail of the oxer.

Sophia has responded to the oxer by producing an extravagant effort. Sensing this, Allison has exaggerated her position. One way we can see this is to look at the angle that Allison's body forms with the ground. That angle is consistent in the first three images, but over the oxer, Allison has closed her hip angle too much. This has interfered with her contact, and the straight line from her elbow to Sophia's mouth is now broken. Over small fences (up to 3-foot-6) you need only come out of the saddle the same amount as when you rise at the posting trot.

poles measured as shown in the diagram on page 24. Trot back and forth several times to show your horse the distance between the poles and to establish his rhythm and balance. You can then raise the fifth rail at **A** to produce a suitable warm-up fence. This obstacle will usually be 18-24 inches (45-60cm). You should now trot through the cavalletti toward the warm-up rail at **A**. Repeat this exercise several times.

As your horse becomes more experienced at cavalletti and gymnastic jumping, you can also add and gradually raise the rail at **B**. Do not make the rail at **B** any higher than the rail at **A** to begin with; once your horse figures out the striding between **A** and **B**, then you can start to raise the rail at **B**.

If I am confident in the progress of the horse and rider involved, I will gradually raise succeeding elements until one element is 3 inches higher than your horse's competitive level. Before adding further obstacles in a gymnastic line, lower the previous element in order to maintain your horse's confidence. When using gymnastics as a training tool, we can make the exercise higher or make it more complex by adding elements, but we should not make the gymnastic higher *and* more complex at the same time. Keep in mind that the performance of your horse is the best judge of how rapidly you can progress in terms of raising the fences.

If this is your horse's first experience with gymnastic jumping or he has limited experience with this type of training, then four to six repetitions through **A** and **B** should be sufficient for your first training period. After an easy day of work on the flat, you can come back and repeat this exercise. If your horse appears to understand what is being asked of him—and especially if he maintains his calmness, balance and regularity through the exercise—then you can change **B** into an oxer with the addition of a second rail in the back pair of standards. The oxer should be no higher than the preceding vertical and only 2 feet wide to start. As usual, once your horse understands the exercise, the height and spread can be raised to the competitive heights and spreads required at that level by the rules.

In order for your horse to see both rails of the oxer, make sure that the front rail of **B** is level with or slightly lower than the back rail. You should then jump these two obstacles several times, entering the four ground poles at a posting trot in the approach to **A,** landing quietly behind the vertical and cantering quietly over the oxer. Jump the oxer at **B** several times before starting to raise and widen it. I usually try to finish the series of repetitions with the last obstacle set at the size and spread that would be required at the horse's level of competition.

Departure

I should add a general comment here about the departure from the obstacle. Riders tend to land thinking about their performance over the obstacle they have just jumped, rather than preparing their horses for the next obstacle. Remember that the departure from one obstacle *is* the approach to the next. Training your horse does not stop the instant he lands over the obstacle. A plan for the departure will help you to re-establish your rhythm and balance. For example, after you jump the oxer at the end of the gymnastic line involved with Gymnastic 2, plan to make a 90-degree turn and halt next to some fixed point in the arena. Al-

> *The exact plan after the obstacle is not so important as the fact that you* have *a plan.*

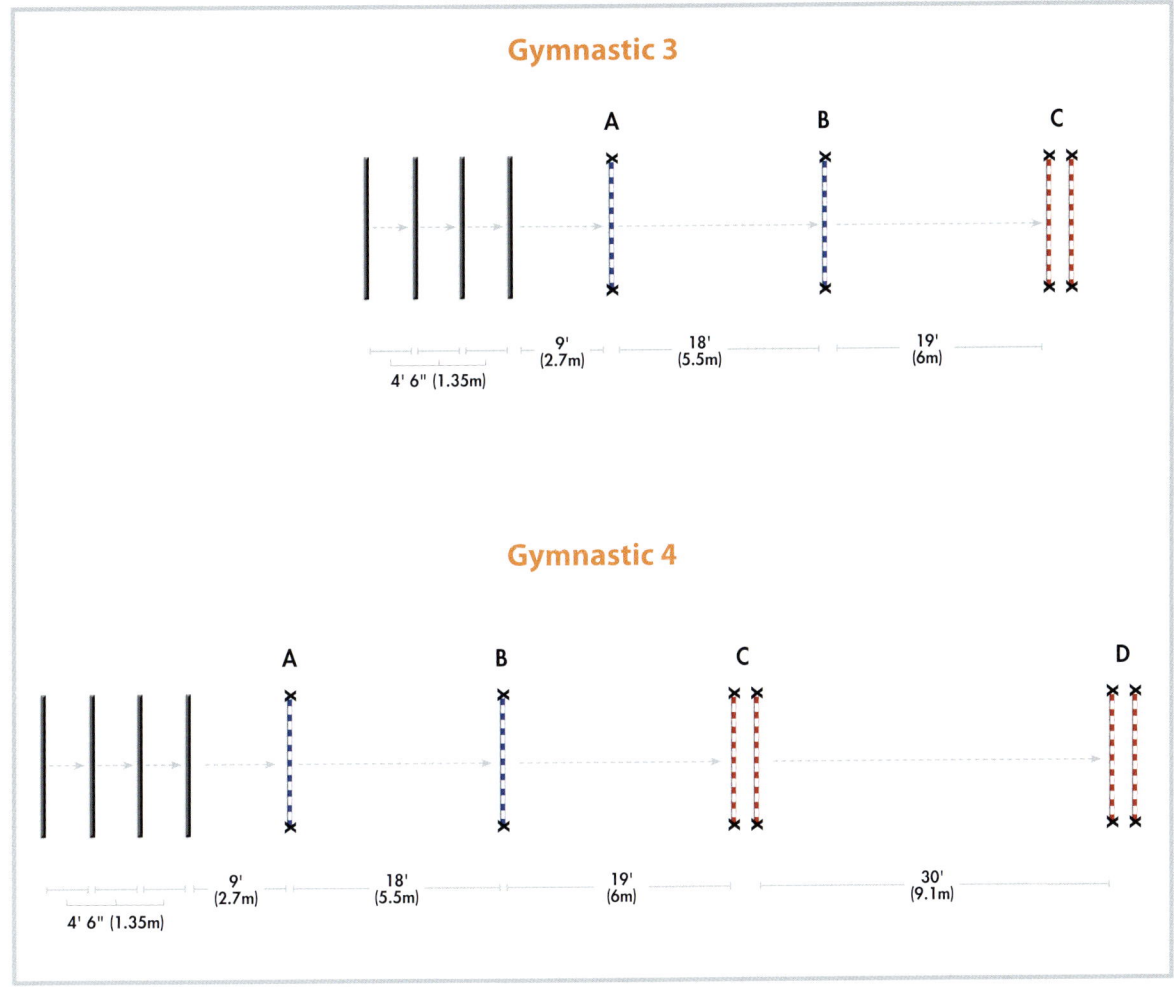

ternatively, you can land and circle after the oxer, counting one, two or three revolutions before making a transition back to trot and approaching the exercise another time. The exact plan after the obstacle is not so important as the fact that you *have* a plan.

Gymnastic 3 (above)

Gymnastic 3 is a continuation of the work that was done in Gymnastic 2 and is created by constructing a vertical at B and adding an oxer 19 feet (6m) from the vertical at B. Start Gymnastic 3 with the rails taken away from **B** and **C**. This will leave only the open standards, four trotting poles and one rail on the ground at **A** as in Gymnastic 2. Warm your horse up as before. Work in both directions through the ground poles. This will introduce variety into your horse's environment and cause him to remain interested later on, when you approach only from one direction.

Repeat the procedure for Gymnastic 2 until you are jumping the obstacles at a comfortable height. If you have raised the vertical at **A** to

⬆ **GYMNASTIC 3** is a simple straight-line exercise, but Darrin Mollett's horse, Beverly's Gamble, is a bit green. As "Gambler" steps into his takeoff at the first vertical, he gives Darrin a "sticky" sensation and Darrin has moved slightly behind the motion to encourage her gelding. While this is an understandable reaction, I prefer the rider to use her legs and—if needed—her stick, rather than her body, to keep her horse in front of her leg.

In the approach to the second vertical, Gambler is more forward and Darrin is in a good position. I especially like the opening of Darrin's elbows, which tells me that the reins are soft and that Gambler is in self-carriage.

Gambler shows his inexperience, however, in the air over the second vertical, where his effort looks more like a sprawl than a jump. Darrin is in balance with her horse, if a bit too high out of the saddle; she has a vertical stirrup leather and a light touch on Gambler's mouth. Gambler looks willing to approach the oxer at the end of the gymnastic line.

Gambler then overjumps the oxer because he does not yet know how to use his body. Although he can obviously jump a bigger fence, he should stay at this gymnastic's present height and spread until he learns to use his body more efficiently. Just because a horse *can* do something does not mean he *should* do it.

slightly higher than your competitive level, you should lower that fence before adding a rail to **B**. For example, set the obstacles in the following manner. The first time that you confront the entire sequence of obstacles they should probably be 2 feet (60cm) at **A**, 3 feet (90cm) at **B** and 3-foot-3 (1m) at **C**, with **C** first set as a vertical. Once your horse is calm and confident, you can make **C** into an oxer that is approximately 3 feet by 3-foot-3 at first.

While I have suggested heights for the various obstacles above, it is up to you to determine

the correct height for your horse's training. The only way you can be sure of the correct height for your horse is to observe his reactions very carefully. If he remains calm, balanced and attentive, you are on the right track. If he becomes agitated and starts rushing or refusing, lower or even remove the last obstacle in the line and continue working quietly and methodically until he re-establishes his mental and physical balance.

If you feel your horse losing confidence as the jumps get higher, immediately lower the obstacles and narrow the spreads until his confidence has returned.

The distance between the three obstacles will produce a one-stride from **A** to **B** and a one-stride from **B** to the oxer at **C**. Remember to strive for balance and regularity. If your horse gets too close to **B** and/or **C,** put a pole on the ground exactly half the distance between **A** and **B** and, again, between **B** and **C**. This will make your horse land sooner after **A** and **B**, thus giving him more distance in front of **B** and **C** to complete his stride. Continue this exercise, gradually raising the heights and spreads as your horse develops fitness and displays regularity and balance through the exercise.

Gymnastic 4 (p. 27)

This gymnastic continues the gymnastics you have worked your horse through before. Work as systematically through it as you did in the preceding ones. In its final form, the gymnastic will require your horse to trot the cavalletti, jump **A**, take one canter stride, jump **B**, take another canter stride, jump the oxer at **C**, land, take two strides and jump the additional oxer marked **D** at the end of the line.

When you increase the technicality of an exercise, you should decrease the height and spread

until you are sure that your horse understands what you want from him. Do not add an obstacle until you are sure your horse understands the problems posed by the one before. If you have raised one of the fences at **A**, **B** or **C** to a marked degree, make sure that you lower it before you add the next obstacle in the line. For practical reasons, I rarely change the spread at **C**, because I would then have to change the distance to **D**. My horses don't seem to mind that I only change the spread of **D** in this exercise.

Gymnastic 5 (p. 34)

Gymnastic 5 is the first time your horse is exposed to a "bounce" gymnastic. By bounce, I mean two or more obstacles set close enough together that your horse will need to land over one element and jump again without taking a stride between them. Bounce fences, sometimes referred to as a "no-stride," are a good agility exercise. Your horse will learn to keep his shoulder in front of him as he jumps and will improve his technique. This is also a good exercise for horses that tend to "rush." (By rush, I mean that your horse increases speed as he gets closer to the obstacle.) Train your horse to keep a steady rhythm in the approach, because when his rhythm is under control, his balance is under control.

Because there is not enough room between the fences for your horse to take a stride, there is not enough time for you to sit down before he jumps again. For this reason, a bounce is also an excellent exercise for you to practice and strengthen your two-point. Have the feeling that your horse tips back and forth over the rails, while you stay poised in your position. Bounces, especially multiple bounces, make you aware of the opening and closing of your elbow. This is an important sensation, as it is the foundation of learning the correct following function of your hands by opening your elbows, not by closing

Beginning Gymnastics 4

⬆ **GYMNASTIC 4** is a continuation of the work you did in Gymnastic 3. Gymnastics in a straight line will develop your horse's confidence and technique, and improve his strength and physical condition. After trotting through the cavalletti, Lisa Mendell and Ridgetop Echo jump in confidently. Lisa is too high out of the saddle, but her legs are in the right place and Echo is obviously concentrating on her job.

Lisa is aware that Echo is small, and she makes sure she takes the correct number of strides between each obstacle. In the second image we can see that Lisa has moved back in the saddle to ensure that she is in a strong position. Because her lower leg is in such a correct place, her upper body is poised over Echo's center of gravity. This security allows her hands and elbows to be soft and elastic.

Echo has jumped the oxer well, and Lisa has stayed with her motion. I would like to see her seat closer to the saddle, but I admire her attitude.

Once your horse is confident about the obstacles and the distance between them, you can use the last oxer to raise his sights (photo inset). You can see that the last oxer in this final image (above) is higher than the preceding three obstacles. When you and your horse have jumped through the gymnastic several times already, you can approach a slightly larger obstacle with confidence as Lisa and Echo are doing here. If you plan to move to the next higher competitive level, gymnastics are a good way to prepare yourself for the higher and wider obstacles you will encounter.

GYMNASTIC 5 will improve your horse's agility, self-carriage and ability to jump multiple efforts without losing his balance. When selecting the photos for this book, I have tried to present you with a wide range of horses. Some were quite experienced; some, like Royal Alyance ("Aly," shown here with Tim Bourke), were quite green. It is possible to teach green horses quite sophisticated gymnastics if—and that is a big "if"—you show your horse one new element at a time. I have compressed Aly's lesson for you, but you will be able to judge the results for yourself. In this book's images, I usually comment equally on the technique of horse and rider; in Gymnastic 5, however, I focus on the horse entirely to make the point that in the first gymnastics you jump, I want you to be an intelligent passenger: Prevent your horse from refusing or running out, and use enough leg to maintain his rhythm, but otherwise let him think for himself. Although an expert rider, in this gymnastic Tim has done an excellent job of being an intelligent passenger.

5a Aly is not experienced, but he has the priceless gift of willingness to go wherever his rider points him. Tim has presented Aly correctly, and Aly is jumping exuberantly, if too high and too loose with his forelegs. This part of the gymnastic is familiar to Aly, because I started many of my earlier gymnastics the same way.

5b Look at Aly's face: He is saying to himself, "What the heck?" But his generous nature is on display. This vertical corresponds to A in the graphic on page 34. We repeated this part of the gymnastic in both directions until he was comfortable before we added the next part of Gymnastic 5. If I needed to, I was ready to call it a day as soon as Aly became puzzled or unwilling. You must copy that attitude with your horse.

Each horse will react differently to circumstances, and you must adapt your training to them, not to some image in a book.

5c Because the jumps are low (and remained low throughout the training session), Aly's face is starting to relax and become interested in the questions we are putting in front of him. We can continue to put more rails in front of him, as long as he keeps a cheerful attitude about it.

5d Compare this photo with the one taken a few minutes earlier (the second image in this series), when Aly jumped his first vertical with a pole on the ground behind the vertical. His technique continues to show his inexperience, but his balance is improving. Over time, gymnastic work will change the shape Aly takes with his forelegs.

5e A few minutes later, Aly is jumping a double-bounce with a cheerful look on his face and no hesitation in his stride. He is landing over the third vertical obviously looking for more toys to play with.

5f Aly's exuberance continues as he jumps well over the single vertical at **D** and his confidence is unshaken as he approaches the next double-bounce. It is interesting to see that he is learning to engage his hindquarters more, as he prepares to jump **E, F** and **G**. If you ride quietly and sympathetically, gymnastics will teach your horse to jump well. Not bad for a 5-year-old with little jumping experience, huh?

your hip angle. If you practice bounce gymnastics, you will learn to maintain vertical stirrup leathers and a quiet, stable upper body.

Note: This is the first gymnastic where I do not utilize a full set of cavalletti before the first obstacle. I plan to gradually remove the poles on the ground as the expertise of horse and rider improves. Eventually, you should be able to trot quietly in rhythm and balance to any type of obstacle without any sort of cavalletti or placing pole in front of the obstacle. Also, this is the first gymnastic that you will approach from either direction; at this point I have started to use what I call "symmetrical" gymnastics, meaning that they will work from either direction. This is a very good way to keep your horse from rushing, because he invariably returns to the same gymnastic.

When I add another element to the gymnastic, I want you to approach towards the new part first, so that your horse immediately notices that you have changed his environment. Inexperienced horses will tend to focus on the change in the exercise, regardless of when it occurs in the jumping sequence. If you approach with the new element as the last in the sequence, many times your horse will make a mistake at elements he successfully negotiated earlier because he is overfocusing on the new element at the end of the sequence. Once he has jumped it, he will usually accept it and you can now use the gymnastic in both directions. However, each time I change a symmetrical gymnastic, I will approach it heading towards the new element first.

Start this gymnastic with one rail on the ground between the standards at **A**, and place a ground pole 9 feet from the rail on the ground between the standards. This ground pole 9 feet away from an obstacle is often referred to as a "placing rail," because its function is to place your horse's takeoff point correctly. After trotting back and forth over the two poles, set **A** at 2 feet (60cm). Jump several times at the trot,

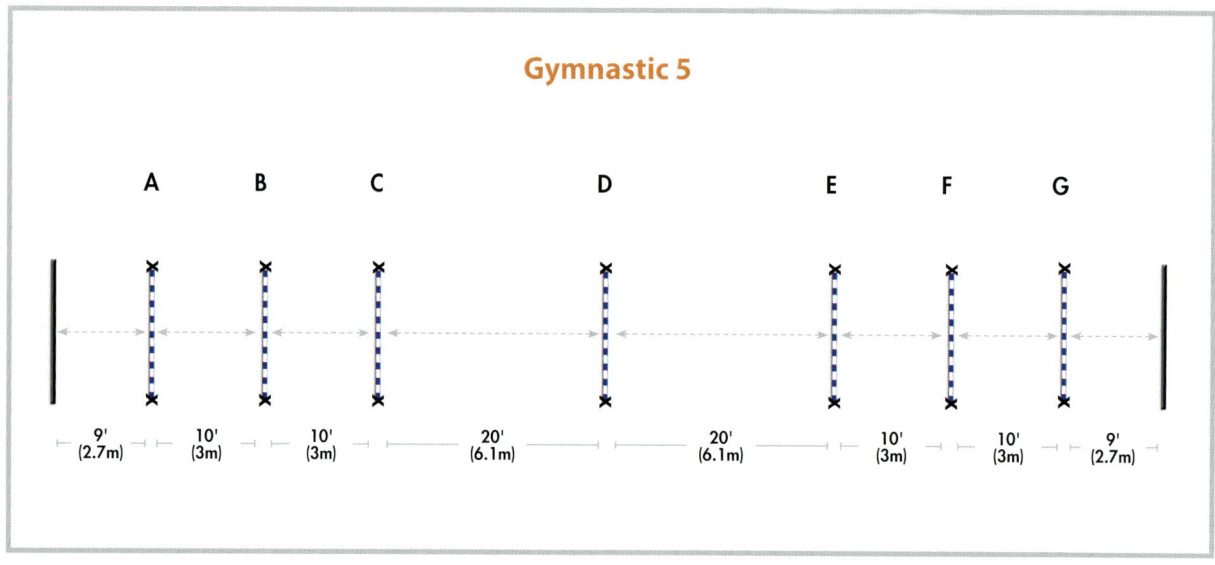

approaching the placing rail, taking two steps after the placing rail and jumping the obstacle at **A**, then reverse and work in the opposite direction.

This means that you will be approaching the obstacle through a line of open standards towards a vertical set at 2 feet (60cm) high, with a placing pole on the ground 9 feet (2.7m) *behind* the obstacle. Your horse should approach at the trot, jump the vertical, land at the canter and step over the 9-foot (2.7m) placing pole without either attempting to put in a stride or attempting to land beyond the placing pole. This is an introductory technique that will teach him how to "bounce" between obstacles.

Occasionally a horse will be startled by the placing pole on the ground behind the obstacle, and will either refuse or overjump badly. If he refuses, lower the obstacle until he will step over it and then raise it in small increments until he will jump the obstacle at its original height.

If your horse overjumps and lands beyond the placing pole, move it out until he *must* land before the placing pole. You can then gradually move the pole back in to 9 feet (2.7m) from the obstacle. Make sure that you repeat this exercise until your horse understands it, as this phase is essential to teaching him to jump a bounce well and to lower his head and neck in the air.

Once you and your horse are confident over this part of the gymnastic in either direction, place a second obstacle the same size as **A** in the standards at **B**. Trot back and forth several times, both from the placing rail into the bounce and back from the bounce to the placing rail. Once your horse is calm and balanced, you can add a rail at **C**. When I first introduce horses to this gymnastic, I rarely make the obstacles more than 2 feet high. Repeat in both directions with a rail at **C** several times and then you can continue to **D**, again with the rail at **D** set about 2 feet high.

Approaching at the trot towards the placing pole before **A**, your horse will now double-bounce A to B and B to C, take one stride at the canter and jump **D**. When your horse jumps from **A** to **D** well and trots calmly from **D** back to **A**, build **E, F** and **G** at the same dimensions and distances. You should build this part of the gymnastic all at once in order to cut down on the total number of repetitions. Because the obstacles at **E, F** and **G** are new to your horse, approach towards **G** first. Once he realizes that the question is the same, you can approach from either direction.

When you have constructed the entire gymnastic, your horse will approach the first placing pole at the trot, jump the first obstacle, bounce, bounce again, land, take one stride in the 20-foot (6.1m) distance, jump the first vertical, take a stride in the next 20-foot (6.1m) distance to the second vertical, land and take another stride in the 20-foot distance, bounce, bounce again, and canter out over the last 9-foot (2.7m) rail on the ground. Concentrate on maintaining your position throughout the exercise so that the horse's back can move freely underneath you. Remain poised in your two-point position during the bounce efforts and return to a light three-point position during the one-stride parts of the gymnastic.

If you are having trouble with your position, use a neck strap to hold yourself in the two-point

When I add another element to the gymnastic, I want you to approach towards the new part first, so that your horse immediately notices that you have changed his environment.

position. Concentrate especially on keeping a light, supple contact with your horse's mouth by relaxing your elbow. This double-bounce gymnastic causes your horse's head and neck to move back and forth in a pronounced fashion. Relaxing your elbows will help you to learn how to maintain a consistent contact throughout the five phases of his jumping effort.

One final comment: The motions of your horse's head and neck when he jumps are not forward and back but rather **back**, forward and back. In order to stay connected with the contact, remember that your elbow must come back towards your body as your horse coils onto his hocks, and then your elbow should come forward to follow your horse as he stretches his neck forward into the jumping motion. This motion should be confined to your elbows, while your upper body remains poised in the two-point position.

I mentioned earlier that this gymnastic is a good exercise to correct horses that rush. The most important part of it is the double bounce. Your horse can rush through a single bounce and land running, but he will find it very difficult to rush through double bounces. Horses learn very quickly to keep their shoulders in front of them when going through this gymnastic, which teaches them to keep their balance.

As a variation, you can remove the rails at **C** and **E**. This will now produce a bounce, two strides to a vertical and two strides to a bounce sequence. Furthermore, if you remove the vertical at **D**, you will then have a bounce, three stride, bounce sequence. However, the more strides you allow for your horse between obstacles, the more time there is for an untrained horse to change the length and rhythm of his strides.

Gymnastic 6 (p. 38)

Gymnastic 6 is an important step in the education of your horse because it is the first time that we ask him to display some flexibility in the length of his stride. This gymnastic requires that you build three different exercises. It is possible to build the three exercises one at a time, but you would then lose the effect on your horse of the different distances and shapes being used one after another. In my opinion, using the three exercises all at the same time—rather than one exercise at a time—helps teach your horse to be more flexible in the length of his stride.

Proceed here as in Gymnastic 2 (page 24). Because I have substantially increased the complexity of the questions in the next few examples, I have placed cavalletti in front of some of them. This will help your horse enter the exercises in a good rhythm and balance. Trot your horse over the cavalletti in both directions. Once he is settled into a rhythm, build the vertical at **A** and later add **B**. As usual, start with the obstacles at around 2 feet. Make sure your horse understands the

question before raising the obstacles. Note that you will now be proceeding only from the cavalletti to the obstacles.

Build the obstacles at **C-D** and **E-F** before you start work. Place a diagonal pole across the *top* of each oxer. I refer to oxers shaped like this as "low-wide oxers." I usually start with the oxers set at 18 inches high and 3 feet wide; however, later in the lesson they will get rather wide. As you change the width of the low-wide oxers it is very important that you remember to keep the distance between **E** and **F** the same, moving the *outside* standards of each oxer to adjust the spread. While the spread of the low-wides will change, their height will remain the same throughout the exercise, with the distance set at 32 feet.

There is always a possibility of the horse "setting down" and putting his feet between the two rails of the oxer, especially when you later combine a low-wide oxer with bounces. Although this is a concern, we can prevent your horse from thinking that the oxer has become a

⬆ **GYMNASTIC 6A-B** is an important step in the gymnastic progression. This is the first of my gymnastics where you will actively communicate with your horse as opposed to being an intelligent passenger. In addition, you now have three gymnastic lines built in the arena, and you should plan to use all three lines during each training session. Tim Bourke and Alyance are starting their session over a gymnastic they have already jumped successfully, one that is similar to Gymnastic 2. Doing this line is not an absolute necessity, but I strongly prefer to have my horse jump a gymnastic he is comfortable with before I ask him for something new.

"Aly" is confident as he trots through the cavalletti poles, and Tim is correct in his position. Although Tim's reins are slightly long, I do not mind that when first schooling young horses through gymnastics. Tim is slightly ahead of Aly's motion as they jump the vertical.

Aly is green and short-strided and he has found the distance to the oxer to be long, causing him to produce a flat arc. Tim has overreacted with his upper body, and is too far out of the saddle. If this problem continues, I will shorten the distance between the vertical and the oxer, which will produce a rounder bascule. The work Tim and Aly are about to undergo in the next two lines will help improve the flexibility of Aly's stride. You can see the **C** and **D** elements of the next gymnastic in the background of these images.

bounce by using a diagonal pole rested across the top of the oxer rails. This helps your horse realize he needs to jump the whole thing (see lower right photo on page 89).

Once you have set the three lines of exercises, unless you have a knockdown, your gymnastic is ready to ride.

After trotting several times through the cavalletti and obstacles at **A** and **B**, trot in both directions over **C-D** with the verticals set at about 24 inches (60cm) high. The distance inside **C-D**, 16 feet (4.9m), is a slightly short stride for a normal horse when approaching at the trot. This part of the exercise will teach your horse to shorten his stride before he jumps.

When trotting back and forth through **C-D** or **D-C**, note that I now place only one ground pole 9 feet in front of each vertical. Eventually, you should be able to jump obstacles from the trot without cavalletti or placing poles, but for now the addition of one pole on the ground will help you maintain the regularity of the trot in the last two or three steps before the takeoff. Your horse should jump the first vertical at **C-D** normally. As his front feet touch the ground behind the first vertical, land in a light three-point position, squeeze the reins without pulling back and use your voice, asking him to slow down. The action of your hands should be like squeezing a sponge, not like pulling on a rope. Your legs should remain in contact with his sides; keep your heels soft and passive. Remember to wait for your horse to take a full stride before jumping again.

Your sensation should be that of slow motion rather than increasing rapidity as you jump out of **C** or **D**. Repeat **C-D** several times in both directions until you are quite sure that your horse is adept at trotting over obstacles at least 3 feet (90cm) high, 16 feet (4.9m) apart, producing one short stride each time. If your horse bounces out instead of taking a short stride, put a pole on the ground halfway between the verticals.

Now proceed to the oxers set at **E-F**

as illustrated on the facing page. These should be no more than 18 inches (45cm) high, but 3 feet (90cm) wide, set 32 feet (9.7m) apart.

With very talented and experienced horses, these oxers can be 2 feet (60cm) high and up to 6 feet (1.6m) wide, still with diagonal rails across the top. Low-wide oxers produce a beneficial stretching of the topline and lowering of the head and neck, which will improve your horse's bascule. This gymnastic exercise produces quite a long two-stride result.

Approach **E-F** at a slightly strong trot with your reins very soft. The oxers are set purposefully quite low. Do not worry about knocking the oxer down, but rather concentrate on getting across the distance between the oxers in two strides. For example, as your horse leaves the ground at the first oxer at **E**, close your heels and think to yourself that you are riding across a ditch rather than jumping an oxer. As you land, your action is the reverse of landing at **D**. Now you must close your heels, "cluck" to your horse, make sure that your rein contact is soft and urge

GYMNASTIC 6C-D I am firmly convinced that horses must be trained to recognize their distance and react to it, especially when the distance is not optimal. Gymnastic 6 is designed to produce a short stride between **C** and **D**. You can tell Aly is inexperienced, because he is jumping too big over **C** into a short distance. This is a mistake, but it is better that he makes this mistake in a controlled situation, rather than later in his career over a solid obstacle. Tim has sensed his predicament, and has taken a hold of Aly's mouth. Due to the long reins I mentioned earlier, Tim's elbows are too far back to be truly effective. At the last moment, Aly recognizes the situation and extricates himself, but he jumps over his shoulders as he does it. Look at the difference in the way Aly uses his shoulders over the first vertical as opposed to the second. Horses do not like this sensation and will usually react to the shorter distance by shortening their stride the next time through.

However, not all horses figure this gymnastic out on their own. If this is the case with your horse, put a ground pole exactly between the two verticals. This will cause him to land sooner after the first vertical, thus giving him more room for his takeoff in front of the second. Unlike the question posed by **A–B**, the exercises at both **C–D** and **E–F** are designed to be jumped in both directions.

⬆ **GYMNASTIC 6E-F** I mentioned earlier that these gymnastics are the first to require some communication from you to your horse. At **E-F,** the third component of the gymnastic, Aly has overjumped the first low-wide oxer. Tim realizes this, and vigorously closes his leg as they land. This causes a slight displacement of Tim's lower leg, but it gets the message across that he and Aly need to go, and they need to go now. Aly has responded correctly to Tim's aids and has increased the engagement of his hind legs. This is important, because Aly can take a longer stride, yet keep the lightness and mobility of his shoulders. This gymnastic is new to Aly, and he has not yet discovered how to adjust his shape over obstacles of different shapes, heights and spreads. Until he learns how to handle his own body, I will not increase the heights or spreads of these gymnastics. He will tell us when it is time to make them more difficult.

your horse forward in two strides, jumping across **E**'s second oxer.

From the trot, 32 feet (9.7m) is a quite long distance, and I find that many horses tend to "chip in" a third stride during the first couple of attempts. You may support your leg with your whip at the point of takeoff in front of the first oxer if necessary. If this correction is successful, repeat this exercise at **E-F** several times in both directions. If my horse cannot reach the second low-wide oxer in two strides, I will attempt this exercise several times, using stronger aids. However, at some point you may have to shorten the distance between E and F until your horse can produce two strides. Once you are successful, stop the exercise for the day. When you return to it, start with the distance where your horse was successful, and then gradually lengthen the distance between the low-wide oxers. The measurement of this exercise is very complex; every time

you change some part of it, you will probably need to adjust the remaining elements.

Practice this long distance until your horse gives you the sensation that he is starting to anticipate and moving forward of his own accord. No one can tell you how many times you will need to repeat this exercise until your horse understands it. My observation is that a very hot, quick-moving Thoroughbred will understand it almost instantly. On the other hand, sluggish, cold-blooded horses may need quite a bit of exposure to it before they fully understand the concept. For each horse, you should notice that between the low-wide oxer elements and the vertical elements, one of them will feel easy and one will feel uncomfortable. This will tell you whether you need to emphasize lengthening or shortening your horse's stride more.

Once you know this, you can start to design exercises that will help you deal with your horse's particular problems. For example, if your horse rushes, you should work from **A** to **B,** and then turn back to **C-D**, rather than allowing him to accelerate through the long distance at **E-F**. A horse that rushes and anticipates a long distance should be allowed to practice long distances occasionally but should not be continually exposed to that particular problem. On the other hand, if your horse is sticky, you should emphasize **A-B** and then **E-F**. There is a natural tendency to practice exercises that you and your horse feel comfortable with. Instead, emphasize the exercises your horse finds more difficult. Practice jumping on a steady stride, a short stride and a long stride until you feel comfortable with any variation in your horse's stride.

For each horse, you should notice that between the low-wide oxer elements and the vertical elements, one of them will feel easy and one will feel uncomfortable.

So Far, So Good

This series of gymnastics does not necessarily have to be done from Gymnastic 1 to Gymnastic 6, but there is logic and a natural progression involved in their development. This logic will help you educate your horse. If you do the exercises in the order they are presented—at least the first time you introduce them to your horse—you will make more rapid progress. Following this, you should not be afraid to go back from time to time and repeat some of the exercises as needed.

Once you feel that your horse handles these gymnastics easily, you can increase their difficulty by increasing the height and spread of the obstacles involved without altering the distances. Throughout the gymnastic training of your horse, your chief goal is to ensure that he remains calm and balanced. If you can do this, you are well on your way to maximizing his full potential.

5
Advanced Jumping

Once your horse has done all of the gymnastics in Chapter 4, he is ready for more complex questions. These will help you both continue to develop your flexibility, control and skill.

Hundreds of books have been written about what constitutes a well-trained horse and how to train a horse to that level. I have read some of them, and the bibliography on page 109 will give you a list of some good books to read, if you want to continue your studies. However, having a well-trained horse comes down to this: If you soften your hands and close your legs and your horse surges forward, that is a good sign. When you soften your legs and squeeze your hands and your horse slows down, that is also a good sign. If you press with one leg against your horse's body and he steps away from the pressure, that is also a good sign. If you soften one hand and squeeze the other and your horse turns toward the firmer hand, that is a very good sign.

When your horse does all of these things calmly and consistently, and can jump obstacles that are suitable in size and type for you both without his losing mental or physical balance, then he is well-trained.

Gymnastic 7 (p. 46)

In Gymnastic 7, you will combine the skills that you practiced in Gymnastic 6, but in one connected series of obstacles rather than as a single short exercise or a single long exercise, as previously. The intention of this gymnastic is that the horse will approach in balance, jump in balance, land in balance and jump again. The horse should land behind the second vertical at **B** and take a slightly long stride to a low, wide oxer at **C**. This will cause him to elongate his body. Immediately upon landing behind **C**, he needs to shorten his stride to deal with the slightly compressed distance between the low, wide oxer and the last vertical at **D**.

To begin work in Gymnastic 7, take away all of the rails until you have your usual five warm-up ground poles. (The fifth ground pole will become the rail for the first obstacle when you raise it.) When your horse is calm and relaxed trotting through the ground poles, use the fifth ground pole to build your usual 18-inch to 2-foot warm-up fence at **A**. Once your horse is settled in over this obstacle, raise **A** in 6-inch (15cm) increments until you have raised the rail at least a total of 1 foot (30cm). There is no rule for the number of repetitions you should have at each level. This number varies from horse to horse and will vary according to the fitness level of the horse in question. Basically, if your horse understands the exercise and handles it in a quiet rhythm, you should be ready for the next level of difficulty. You can either raise the element or add an additional element. If your horse is competing in show jumping or eventing, you should raise **A** until it reaches the height of your competitive level.

When your horse has jumped this obstacle to your satisfaction, walk and let him relax. Set the rail at **A** back to 2 feet (60cm) and add a rail at **B** starting at 2 feet (60cm), gradually raising it to 3-foot-6 (1.06m), increasing it in 6-inch (15cm)

Advanced Jumping 5

GYMNASTIC 7 develops the flexibility of your horse's stride and improves his ability to quickly react to obstacles of different size and shape. In order to be candid about this horse's performance, I will call her "Greenbean." She is not here to defend herself, and I do not want to insult her, especially when she was obviously trying to understand the questions posed by this gymnastic. Horses like this remind us that there are few limits to what our horses can learn, if only we have patience and the ability to find a way to explain to the horse what it is that we want him to do.

Darrin Mollett and Greenbean jump well into the gymnastic, although Greenbean already shows her inexperience with her loose jumping style. At the peak of the bascule, I like to see horses form a three-sided "box" with their forelegs and their forearms above the horizontal. In contrast to that imaginary model, Greenbean's forearms are below the horizontal and her forelegs are very loose under her shoulders.

Greenbean has tightened her form over the second vertical—but she tells us she is still on her forehand at takeoff, because she has drawn her feet back under her chest rather than lifting her knees forward and up. This shape is caused by too much weight on your horse's forehand as he takes off.

The distance from the second vertical to the low-wide oxer is quite long and Darrin is softening her elbows and closing her heels, telling Greenbean to lengthen her stride to the next obstacle.

This image over the oxer is taken too late for us to judge Greenbean's style in the air, but she understands this part of the exercise; she is stretching out and looking for her landing. Darrin is centered above her effort, if a bit too high out of the saddle.

I suspect that Greenbean will take the same shape over the last vertical that she did over the first two. She is on the forehand at the point of takeoff, which usually affects the shape we see in the air a split second later. Darrin is in the right place: Her legs are at the girth, her reins are soft and she has a light three-point position in the saddle.

The usual answer to a question about a horse that "hangs" his front legs (takes an inefficient shape) in the air is to shorten the distance between obstacles, hoping that the horse will learn to shift more weight to his hindquarters before the takeoff. It is true that the horse with more weight in his hindquarters than his forehand will take a better shape in the air. However, when dealing with horses that hang their forelegs I get better results if I first school through low-wide oxers before shortening the distance between verticals. The stretching caused by the spread seems to unlock the horse's shoulders, while the longer distances activate his hindquarters. (The parallels between low-wide oxers for jumping and working your dressage horse in a long and low frame are worthy of an entire book, but that is a topic for another time.)

increments. After several repetitions at 3-foot-6 (1.06m), give your horse another period of rest. Obviously, if your horse is competing at lower levels, you should adjust the obstacles to suit those lower requirements.

Put the rail at **B** down to a lower height, probably 6 inches lower than the maximum height for the competitive level of your horse. When you build the low-wide oxer at **C**, remember to put a diagonal rail across it as you did for the previous gymnastic. Set the low-wide oxer at only 18 inches in height but with a spread of 3 feet (90cm). Now trot through the cavalletti, jump the obstacle at **A**, take one long canter stride and jump **B** (this part of the gymnastic is similar to the work you did in earlier exercises). When you land over **B** soften your reins, close your legs and lengthen your horse's stride. The aids that you use between **B** and **C** are the same aids that you used in Gymnastic 6, jumping exercise E-F (page 38).

If your horse responds correctly, you should take one stride in this 20-foot (6.1m) distance between **B** and **C**. Practice this gymnastic from the cavalletti to **A, B** and **C** several times, making the spread of the oxer 6 inches (15cm) greater each time. You should be able to jump an 18-inch (45cm) oxer with a 5-foot (1.5 m) spread quite easily. It is very important that you change the spread of the oxer by adjusting the back rail and not the front; do not alter the distance between **B** and **C** when you change the width of the oxer.

After a period of rest, narrow the spread of the oxer at **C** to 4 feet (1.2m). Add a rail in the standards at **D**, set about 2-foot-6 (75cm) high. Make sure that the distance to **D** from the back of the oxer at **C**, as it is now set, is 19 feet (5.8m). Each time you change the back rail of the oxer at **C**, you should adjust the distance to **D** to maintain the same amount—that is, 19 feet (5.8m). I typically increase the width of the low-wide oxer in 6-inch increments, and I change the distance from **C** to **D** each time I change the width. Once your horse easily handles the wider spread followed by a vertical on a slightly short stride, I then usually raise the last vertical, again using 6-inch (15 cm) increments. If your horse understands this exercise at these heights and spreads, I will leave

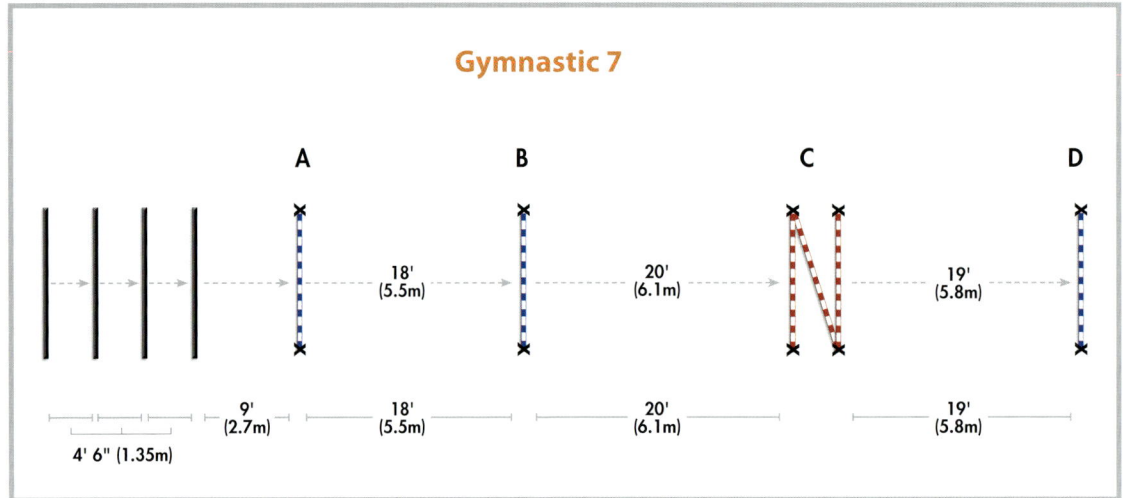

Gymnastic 7

C and D set and raise the vertical at B. Raising the vertical at B has a couple of desirous effects: The steeper arc required by the taller vertical prevents horses from being slightly strung out at C. If B and C are too low, the horse could "sprawl" through the distance between C and D, lessening the effect of the low-wide oxer. Raising B also makes the distance between C and D seem slightly longer.

Because I try to change this exercise slightly each time the horse comes through it, the ground person is going to get quite a workout during this exercise, raising, lowering, and remeasuring after each repetition.

You now will trot in over the cavalletti, jump A, land, take a normal stride, jump B, then land and extend in your stride to C. Following C, shorten your horse's stride in order to jump D correctly. The aids used between C and D are the same aids that you used in Gymnastic 6 at C-D (page 38), where you shortened your horse's stride between two vertical elements. Gymnastic 7 is more difficult than Gymnastic 6, but it is not impossible for the normal horse. Your horse should know how to expand his stride and jump a wide fence from a long distance and then immediately return to balance and compress his stride in order to jump another obstacle from a shorter distance.

After your horse has satisfactorily jumped this gymnastic, you can raise D, again in 6-inch (15cm) increments, until he can eventually jump from 3-foot-6 to 4 feet (1.06m-1.2m) at D, if that is the required height of his competitive level. After one or two repetitions of this entire gymnastic, a horse jumping in 3-foot-6 (1.06m) classes or eventing at 3-foot-6 (1.06m) should be able to come through this gymnastic with the obstacles set at 3 feet (90cm) at A, 3-foot-6 (1.06m) at B, 2 feet (60cm) high by 5 feet (1.5m) wide at C, and 3-foot-6 (1.06m) at D. However, the first time you attempt this gymnastic, do not be too enthusiastic with the height and spread.

Gymnastic 8 (p. 50)

Gymnastic 8 is your first introduction to changing direction in a gymnastic. Previously, all of your gymnastics have been in a straight line, and by now your horse should have developed considerable proficiency in expanding and contracting his stride. However, modern course design places great emphasis on flexibility of direction as well as flexibility of stride. Therefore we must use gymnastics to develop lateral flexibility in the same way that we used gymnastics to develop longitudinal flexibility.

To construct this gymnastic, place a rail on the ground and build a vertical fence 9 feet (2.7m) behind that, followed by an oxer 18 feet (5.5m) away as shown. In the diagram, these are obstacles A and B. When you begin your training over this gymnastic, set A at your usual 18-inch to 2-foot height. As you proceed, the oxer at B can be set at the same low height to start if your horse is green; in case your horse is very experienced, you should still not start with B any higher than a 2-foot-6 spread. Once he understands the new gymnastic, you can raise B, and indeed the succeeding obstacles, to his competitive level.

Once your horse is settled in over A and B, measure in a straight line 50 feet (15.2m) and assemble the components you will need to construct an oxer as shown at E. For now, however, while you leave the standards in place, put the rails for E on the ground to the side so that you can ride in a straight line through the open standards at E.

Build **C** and **D** so that the left standard of **C** and the right standard of **D** are on the imaginary straight lines (as indicated by the dotted lines in the diagram on page 50) formed by measuring the 50-foot distance to the left and right standards of **B** and **E**.

The relationship of the obstacles at **C** and **D** is critical to your success with this exercise, so be very precise in your measurements. As always, use a tape. Measure 38 feet (11.6m) from the right end of the pole at **B** to the right end of the pole at **C**. Turn the pole at **C** until its left standard is on the straight line between the right standards of **B** and **E**. Set the height at 18 inches to 2 feet (60cm) to start. You will have to "slide" the vertical at **C** until you have the left standard of **C** on the imaginary dotted line **BCE**, 38 feet between the right-hand standard of **B** and **C**, and the vertical at **C** set on a 45-degree angle to the imaginary dotted line. It will take a little adjustment to satisfy all three of these requirements. Later, you will need to go through a similar process when you build the vertical at **D**.

Repeat this process to build the obstacle at **D**, measuring 26 feet (7.3m) from the left end of the pole at **B** to the left end to the pole at **D**. Set the height as at **C**. Do not measure from the ends of the wings (if used), as their widths may vary. If you have constructed this exercise correctly, the right standards at **A** and **B** will form a straight line with the left standard of **C** and the right standard of **E**. In addition, that straight line will be parallel with the long side of the arena, if you are working in an enclosed arena. Make sure the left standards

Advanced Jumping

GYMNASTIC 8 teaches your horse skills he will need to handle courses well. If you can select the lead that your horse will land on, you have a better chance of arriving at the next fence in rhythm and balance. Full Moon Rising (Millie) tends to drift to the left, so Tim Bourke is insisting that she jump to the right instead. He has applied his left leg quite strongly, which explains Millie's overreaction over the oxer (shown as **B** in the page 50 diagram). Tim can feel that Millie still wants to go to the left, so he has exaggerated his right opening rein.

As Millie begins to understand the gymnastic, Tim's aids become subtler. Both horse and rider are poised and balanced between **B** and the vertical at **C**. In the last image, Millie has accepted the change of direction and is concentrating on her takeoff.

Practice this gymnastic until you can select your horse's landing stride every time. Next, ask your horse to land on the left lead after **C**. You will find it difficult to change your aids that quickly, from asking for the right lead over **B**, to asking for the left lead as your horse prepares to jump **C**.

Remember to work through this gymnastic in the other direction—landing on the left lead after the oxer and proceeding to the vertical shown as **D** in your graphic on page 50. Your horse will show a preference for one lead over the other. Make a habit of practicing his weak side more than his strong side, until your horse becomes ambidextrous.

of **A**, **B**, right standard of **D**, and left standard of **E** form a similar straight line. You may have to struggle with the alignment of this exercise a little, until you get everything absolutely symmetrical, but this will help you to develop the correct attitude towards all your gymnastic work. A little extra time spent aligning your exercises will tend to produce horses that are symmetrical.

Warm up as usual and then begin work at the trot, with a placing pole 9 feet (2.7m) from **A** on the ground. When you are satisfied that your horse is warmed up and prepared, you may now jump from **A** to **B** to **C**. However, before you put the three elements together, I want you to trot over the obstacle at **C** as a single jump. Once you have done this, it will come as no surprise to your horse when you then ask him to jump **A**, **B** and **C**. With very inexperienced horses, I will first merely place the rail on the ground at **C**, and I will not raise it until that horse has stepped over it once. This will increase his confidence, and ensure that he already has the correct answer when we start to raise the rail at **C**.

When doing a course, it is a terrific advantage for you to be able to select which lead your horse will land on after a jump. To practice this skill, use the following technique: As your horse takes off at **B**, open your right rein and move your left rein over to the right so that it exerts a slight pressure against your horse's neck. Squeeze with your left leg and shift your weight slightly over your right knee. Turn your head and eyes and look to the center of the vertical at **C**.

This distance should produce three strides from **B** to **C** on a mild curve. Jump **A** to **B** to **C** several times until your horse understands the right turn. Do not obsess if he will not land on his right lead; we will fix that later on. The reason we turned to the right first after **B** is to give your horse an extra stride to "read" the problem. When we go in the opposite direction, your horse will have one less stride to react to the obstacle.

If he misunderstands and runs out at **C**, he will usually refuse by "running out" (refusing)

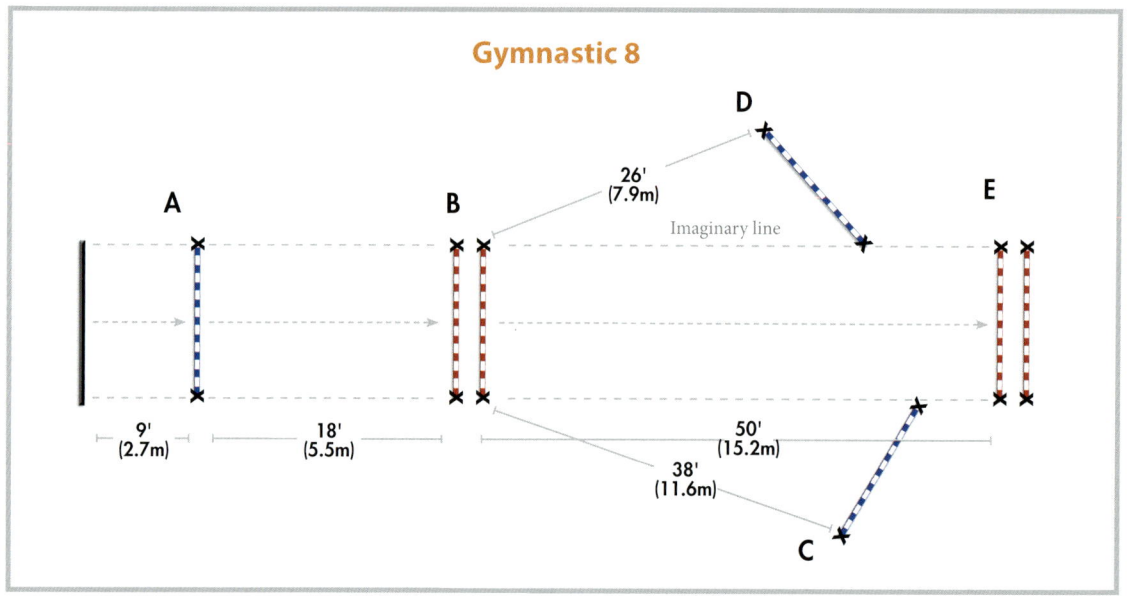

to the left. Take one of the rails on the ground by **E** and construct a wing on the left side of **C**, and then continue with your training. (Remove the wing at **C** later, to make sure your horse is responding correctly to your turning aids.)

Just as with your first attempt at **A, B** and **C**, before you attempt three new obstacles in a row, jump the obstacle at **D** as a single effort. You are in effect "showing" your horse the jump before you ask him to jump it in sequence. You should now jump **A** to **B** to **D**, reversing the aids you used to turn to the right—that is, in front of **B** open the left rein, use your right rein against the neck and close your right leg to press your horse into a curve to the left. Done correctly, your horse should land on the left lead and produce two strides from **B** to **D**. If you were successful landing on your right lead a moment ago, when turning to the right, do not be surprised if you do *not* land on the left lead while turning left. You have discovered something about the imperfect state of your horse's training, which is a fixable problem.

Once again, your horse may duck out—now to the right. This is understandable, as we have just spent five minutes teaching him to jump to the right going from **B** to **C**.

Do not become flustered if your horse runs out to the right at **D**. Take one of the rails from the ground at **E** and make a wing from the right-hand standard of **D**. Repeat the left-hand turning exercise several times. Your horse will quickly come to understand that he should listen to your aids in order to determine which direction he is going to go next. When you are successful, remember to remove the wing to test if your horse now understands both turning aids.

Once horses understand this gymnastic, they become very adept at changing their direction.

With practice, you will find that all you have to do to change direction is to open one rein and look—turning your head and eyes in the new direction—and your horse will seek that fence to the right or the left, according to your actions.

While you give your horse a break, build an oxer at **E**. This oxer should not be too big; 3 feet (90cm) in front and 3-foot-3 (1m) behind, with a 3-foot (90cm) spread, should be sufficient to start. Now, trot into the gymnastic and jump **A** and **B**, then take four slightly steady strides to **E**. The action of your reins on landing after **B** is the same as the action you used to handle the short distance between the verticals at **C-D** in Gymnastic 6 (page 38).

Land behind **B** in a light three-point position with your hands at your horse's wither and close your hands without pulling back. You should feel that you are squeezing a sponge, not pulling on a rope. Do not sit down or lean back and grip with your heels, as this will cause your horse to run through this exercise in three long strides rather than taking the desired four quiet, steady strides from **B** to **E**. Your horse will try to show off what he has learned and wander from **C** to **D**. This is normal and you should repeat **A** to **B** to **E** until he goes straight through. If your horse is "hot," you will only need one or two repetitions before he figures this question out. An intelligent, slightly "hot" horse will wander a bit the first time from **B** to **E**, be quite good the second repetition, and many times will start to rush towards **E** the third time. Your horse is not misbehaving; he is very intelligent, has quickly figured out what you wanted and now wants to show off what he has learned. If this happens, do not fight with him; just go back to turning right or left upon landing after **B**.

Once you have rehearsed all three possible

lines through the gymnastic, you can start to do various courses. For example, approach **A, B** and **C**, and then continue left at the canter over **D** in the opposite direction than when jumping it from the gymnastic at **A** and **B**. (You should have ground lines on both sides of **C** and **D** to facilitate this.) After jumping **D**, return to the trot, approach **A** and **B**, and turn towards **D**. Maintain the right canter lead after **D** and jump **C** in the other direction.

Return to the trot. Jump **A, B** and **E** and quietly pull up to a halt after **E** in a straight line. This pattern now allows you a great deal of variety in your direction and improves your control of your horse's stride.

This pattern becomes quite complex for your horse's mind, and it is natural for him to have some trouble with it at first. If he has difficulty at any point, lower the jumps until he feels comfortable to you again. Most horses will display some form of right- or left-lead preference. This will take some time to correct, and you should be patient in the meantime. He is not acting this way to irritate you, but rather because we have not yet developed his physique completely. You can unbalance your work to help correct a mistake. If your horse has trouble turning to the left, you should emphasize the curve from **B** to **D**. If he has trouble to the right, emphasize the curve to **C**. Occasionally, if your horse is excitable, you can jump **A** and **B**, halt without jumping **C, D** or **E**, reassure him and walk away from the exercise. In general, I do not like pulling event horses or racehorses up in front of obstacles, but I am willing to do it with any type of horse if he is extremely difficult and agitated in the approach, or if I feel in any way the situation is unsafe.

Gymnastic 9 (p. 54)

Gymnastic 9 is a continuation of training your horse to jump on curves. It will teach him how to

Advanced Jumping

↑ GYMNASTIC 9 My students and I call this gymnastic "The Cartwheel." The image farthest from you above, which corresponds to **B** in the graphic on page 54, illustrates correct turning aids. Darrin Mollett has engaged her inside leg at the girth, opened her inside rein, brought her outside rein against the neck, and her eyes are already calculating her path to **C**. We cannot see it in this image, but from the bending in Sophie's body, chances are that Darrin's outside leg is behind the girth and active. Her upper body is a little high out of the saddle for such a small fence.

The next image between **B** and **C** is terrific. Sophie is bent around Darrin's inside leg, and we see the action of the outside leg creating the turn. The rider and the horse are both leaning exactly the same amount, compensating for the centrifugal force of the turn. Darrin's eyes are fixed on her next obstacle, judging the remaining strides before the takeoff.

Although I want you to land a little closer to your saddle than Darrin has after **C** (on the facing page), her outside leg and rein are so correct that Sophie is approaching the third obstacle in this gymnastic bent to the inside. Look at the engagement of Sophie's inside leg, which is the result of Darrin's correct aids. Modern show-jumping courses are so interrelated that your landing over this obstacle is the approach to your next obstacle.

Because her position was quite high landing after **B**, Darrin has lost her balance slightly as she approaches **A**. I suspect her takeoff distance is slightly long to **A** and Darrin has leaned away from the fence in an attempt to lengthen her stride. The correct reaction would be to maintain the position of her upper body and close her legs. When you attempt the cartwheel, keep your shoulder in the same relationship to your knee all the way around the circle. Because Darrin is always looking where she is going, Sophie's footprints form a precise circle around the cartwheel.

be flexible in his length of stride. I call this exercise "The Cartwheel" for obvious reasons. Set the exercise up as shown with the verticals at about 2 feet (60cm). After warming your horse up, trot and canter back and forth over **A**. Then trot and canter your horse back and forth over **B** and **C**, each as individual obstacles.

Now, on a circle at a quiet canter, jump from **A** to **B** to **C** and continue **A** to **B** to **C**, and so on, remaining on the circle for up to six complete revolutions.

At the takeoff in front of each obstacle, use the same aids to turn as you did in Gymnastic 8 (page 50). Open your inside rein, put your outside hand slightly against the withers, place your weight slightly over your inside knee and ankle and look at the center of the next jump.

A normal horse should produce five to six strides from **A** to **B**, three strides from **B** to **C** and five to six strides from **C** to **A**. Eventually your horse should be able to do three or four revolutions around the exercise in both directions without losing his rhythm.

As you work your horse in both directions around the cartwheel, be sure to note which direction causes him more trouble. If you have done Gymnastic 8, you probably already know which direction will cause your horse more trouble. In addition, knowledge of one-sidedness is invaluable information for you in the continuing education and improvement of your horse; for example, if he "pops" his shoulder to the right, you know that you should emphasize right leg yielding and right shoulder-in.

Gymnastic 10 (p. 55)

This is a good gymnastic to teach your horse to keep his balance and to jump on a compressed stride. In addition, the gymnastic has a very calming effect on horses, because you are now going to trot into it from both directions. Eventually, many horses will slow down as they realize they are just going to stop, turn around and jump back in the other direction.

Begin with two rails on the ground 9 feet (2.7m) apart at **A**. Trot back and forth through this several times until, as usual, your horse is calm, relaxed and balanced. Then raise the rail at **A** as shown,

Gymnastic 9

A

30'
(9.1m)

B

24'
(7.3m)

C

making it 18 inches to 2 feet and trot through this several times, stepping over the placing pole 9 feet (2.7m) from **A**, taking two steps, jumping and landing at the canter after the small vertical. After a few repetitions in this direction, trot back the other way so that you are jumping the vertical first and landing, then cantering out over the placing pole. Your horse might be reluctant to jump with the placing pole behind the obstacle. Lower the vertical the first time you jump the exercise with the ground pole behind the vertical, to make sure he understands that there is room behind the obstacle for him to put his feet down. Once he is confident, raise it back to its original height, so that he is jumping the same height in both directions. This is an excellent exercise to teach your horse to jump in a rounder shape and to look where he is going to land. It also is a rehearsal for a bounce, which is nice, because you will soon be jumping bounces again.

Once your horse has accepted this exercise and is ready for further work, place another vertical of the same height 40 feet away from **A**, at **B**. Place a 9-foot (2.7m) ground pole behind **B**. Now then, place additional ground poles 10 feet (3m) behind **A**, and 10 feet in front of **B**. At this point you should have constructed a gymnastic that has two obstacles and four ground poles, set as described above. You can now trot in, land from **A**, take three canter strides and jump out over **B**. The rails on the ground will help maintain the regularity of your horse's stride.

You can practice going from **A** to **B** in three strides; then you can turn around and come back from **B** to **A**, having raised the fence at **A** until it is 6 inches (15cm) higher than the fence at **B**. Quite often I will use this exercise to raise horses' sights a bit and get them jumping a bigger fence than they might otherwise see in their daily course of business. I am reluctant to be explicit about the heights of the rails until I see the reactions of the horses involved; however, your horse should certainly be able to jump the height of his competitive level at the second obstacle (**A** or **B**, according to which direction you attempt the exercise.)

After you have successfully come back and forth from **A** to **B** and **B** to **A**, lower fences **A** and **B** until they are approximately 2-foot-6 to 3 feet (75-90cm) high. Build the vertical at **C** between **A** and **B**, as shown in the illustration below.

Gymnastic 10 teaches your horse to keep his balance while he jumps and improves the use of his head and neck over the jumps.

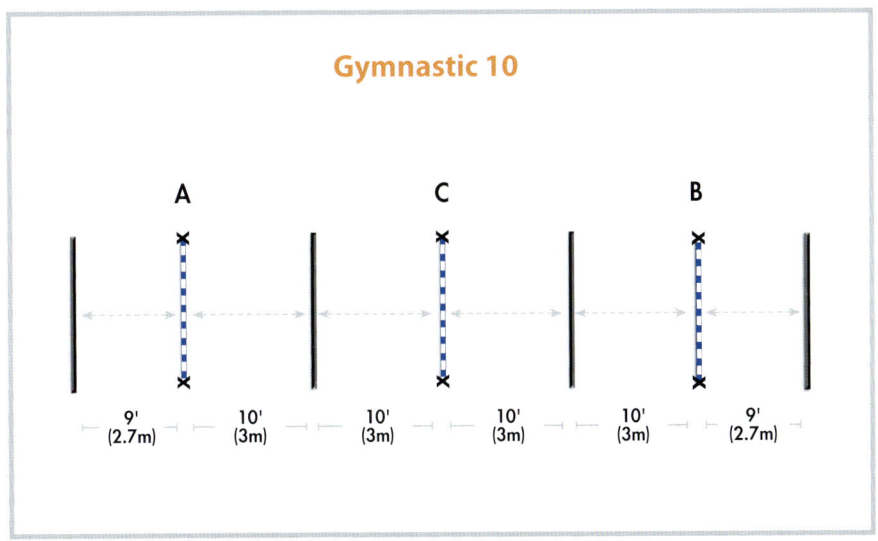

Gymnastic 10

↑ GYMNASTIC 10 teaches your horse to keep his balance while he jumps and improves the use of his head and neck over the jump. Tim Bourke is sitting quietly here, even though Full Moon Rising has slipped into the canter just before the placing pole. This is a sign of tension in "Millie", and the next time we use this gymnastic, I will deal with it by having Tim shorten the length of his approach to the placing pole.

Jumping the first vertical, Tim is well placed but needs to shorten his reins. I approve of long or loose reins when you begin gymnastic work, but as the gymnastics become more complex your connection with your horse should become more sophisticated. Millie understands the question posed by the pole between the first and second vertical, and is looking for her landing.

Because she landed correctly behind the first vertical, Millie has plenty of room in front of the second vertical. She is taking a good shape at the peak of her bascule and lowering her head and neck to look for her next landing. Except for his long reins, Tim has a good position. The distances between the verticals are designed to be comfortable for the average horse, and Tim is going with Millie's stride as she steps up to the third vertical.

Once horses understand this gymnastic, I change the heights of the verticals, one at a time—and if you look carefully, you can see that the three verticals here are not equal in height. The third vertical is lower than the others in this line. Millie has spotted this subtle change, and has made an economical (I might even say unimpressive) effort over it. I view this as a sign of maturity, when a horse accurately measures the height of the obstacle ahead and produces a suitable effort to clear it.

Adjust the three verticals until they are all the same height.

Now you can trot back and forth several times through this exercise. Starting from **A** you can raise **C** 3 inches (7.5cm) and raise **B** 6 inches (15cm), so that your horse has the sensation that he is jumping slightly uphill. Later, you can vary the height of the three verticals, from low to high to low, or vice versa. This is an excellent exercise to teach your horse to look at the height of the jump rather than jumping mechanically over rails of equal heights.

As your horse gains in balance and confidence, you should practice this exercise without the poles on the ground between the verticals.

Be sure to regulate the number of repetitions and the height of the fences so that your horse finishes his workout with enthusiasm and confidence. While the actual number of repetitions will vary according to your horse's fitness, at every stage of fitness you should remember that you are jumping obstacles in quick succession, which is always more fatiguing than jumping obstacles one at a time. In addition, young horses will become mentally fatigued because they are unused to this sort of training. As a general rule, try to stop one repetition before your horse gets tired.

Gymnastic 11 (p. 58)

This gymnastic is an excellent exercise to teach your horse to use his back while jumping. Make sure you do this gymnastic on as soft a rein as possible in order to encourage your horse to use his head and neck. The relationship between height, spread and distance will become quite complex as this gymnastic develops. It is essential that you have a knowledgeable and efficient jump crew to help you during your work through Gymnastic 11.

Begin this gymnastic with two poles on the

ground 9 feet (2.7m) apart. When your horse has settled in, build a vertical at **A**, which I usually set about 18 inches to 2 feet to begin with. After you are satisfied with your horse's relaxation at **A**, change the vertical at **A** into an oxer as shown. Whenever you see a diagonal line across an oxer in one of my illustrations, it means that I want you to make the spread wider than the height, which I refer to as a "low-wide" oxer. For ex-

ample, build this low-wide oxer 18 inches (45cm) high but make it 3 feet (90cm) wide. I use fences of this shape to stretch a horse's topline, to lower his head and neck in the air over the obstacle, and to teach him to push more with his hindquarters.

Trot back and forth over this low-wide oxer until you and the horse are warmed up, comfortable and confident.

Place another low-wide oxer of equal dimen-

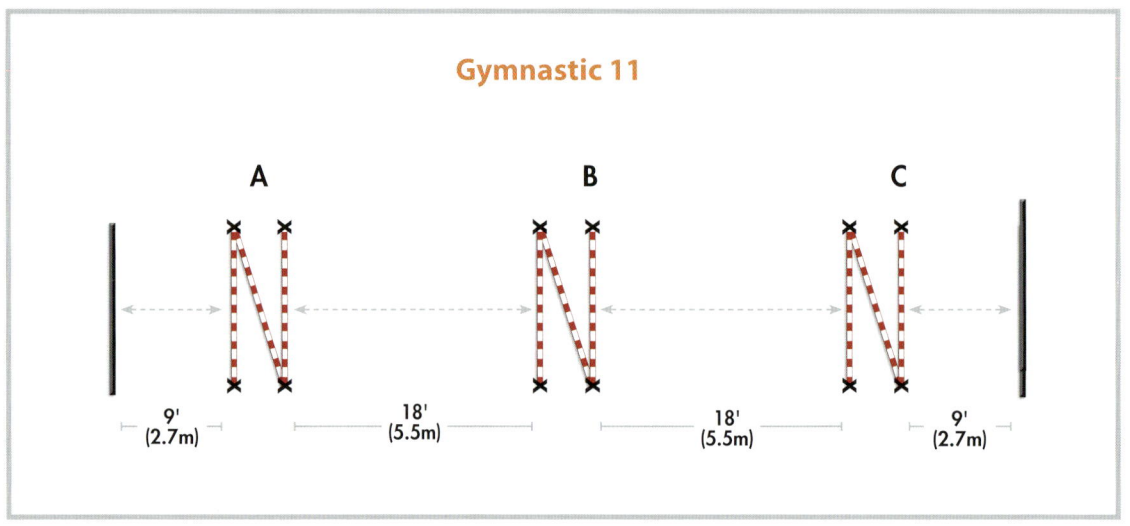

Advanced Jumping 5

GYMNASTIC 11 can be used for a variety of reasons. Set as three low-wide oxers, it teaches your horse to push more with his hindquarters. Later on, you can raise one, some or all of the oxers to teach your horse to take a better shape as he bascules over the obstacles. Because Ridgetop Echo is small and a little green, I have allowed Lisa Mendell to approach the placing pole before the first oxer at a canter. Echo has her ears pricked and is studying the gymnastic intently. Green horses will usually jump too high over the low-wide oxers, as she has done here.

The distances between the oxers is designed to be long. When your horse (like Echo) is barely more than pony-sized, it are really long. Lisa has closed her leg strongly, which has caused her seat to fall back in the saddle. Her soft reins compensate for this minor error, and Echo is not bothered.

Echo over-jumps the second oxer and Lisa is staying with her. Her seat is probably above the saddle the correct amount, but she has closed her hip angle too much to suit me. Over small fences, I want your body to keep the same angle to the ground throughout the gymnastic.

Landing over the second oxer, Lisa is still in a strong position, making sure that Echo goes forward to the third oxer. Her upper body has returned to the correct angle, her lower leg is rock-solid and her elbows have softened. Echo understands exactly what Lisa is talking about, and she responds by overjumping the last oxer. This reaction will dissipate with repetition, and horses will learn to measure their fences accurately regardless of size or shape.

sions as **A**, 18 feet (5.5m) away from **A**, and put a placing pole 9 feet from the low-wide oxer at **B**, on the opposite side from the low-wide at **A**. If you have sufficient jump crew, it is a good idea to jump the placing pole and **B** separately first, while temporarily removing the low-wide oxer at **A**. Your horse will usually immediately understand the question posed by the low-wide oxer at **B**, and you should then jump **B** in reverse, approaching the low-wide oxer from the side with no placing pole and landing between the low-wide oxer and the placing pole.

Once you are sure your horse understands the question in either direction, build the low-wide oxer at **A** again, and approach at the trot from **A** to **B**. Trot over the placing pole, jump the first oxer, land and take one canter stride and jump the second oxer. Jump the gymnastic from **A** to **B** until you are satisfied your horse is confident, and then approach from **B** to **A** until you feel equally satisfied in either direction.

You can now remove the placing pole behind **B** and add another low-wide oxer, 18 feet beyond **B** at **C**, with a 9-foot (2.7m) placing pole behind it. While you should practice back and forth several times, approach from the direction **C-B-A**, so that your horse focuses on the new element first; when he lands he will see low-wide oxers he has already successfully jumped.

If your low-wide oxers have been set at 18 inches (45cm) high by 3 feet (90cm) wide throughout, even an inexperienced horse should find this exercise easy to do and, indeed, may start to rush a bit. If this is the case, it is time for you to start raising the oxers. I raise all of the oxers at once in 3-inch increments and keep the spread the same, at least during your horse's first introduction to this gymnastic; at some point the height of the oxer will become greater than the spread. Until I am sure that the horse understands the question being asked, I will be a bit more conservative with the spreads.

Later on, I increase the spread of the oxers as well as the height. Make sure you maintain the same distance between the obstacles and placing poles. For example, if you change the spread at **A**, you should move the front rail of the low-wide oxer and adjust the placing pole accordingly. If you change the spread at **B**, you should remeasure the entire gymnastic, as this will change the distance between the obstacles. Your helper on the ground will be able to skip his visit to the health club after this session.

You must be aware that this gymnastic quickly changes in nature from quite easy to quite difficult as the interplay of the height, spread and 18-foot (5.5m) distance becomes more complex. It is easy to overface a young horse by asking him to do too much in this gymnastic. If you make a mistake, it should be that you are too conservative rather than too aggressive in raising the heights and spreads.

Gymnastic 12 (p. 61)

Gymnastic 12 teaches your horse to look at the top rail of the next obstacle, and to adjust his effort accordingly. By alternatively raising or lowering either the two verticals or the low-wide oxer, you can teach your horse to focus on the upcoming question and to think about what he is going to do next, rather than rushing through a series of obstacles that are all set at the same height.

Begin Gymnastic 12 with two poles on the ground 9 feet (2.7m) apart. Once your horse is comfortable, build a 2-foot vertical at **A** as shown and trot into this several times. Eventually, approach at the trot from both directions so that your horse is comfortable going either way.

Now build the oxer at **B**. Start with the oxer about 2 feet high and 3 feet wide. Again, note the diagonal lines across the oxer in the diagram. This means that the spread is greater than the height, and the height of this oxer is quite low.

Trot from the vertical to the oxer, **A** to **B**, and then later on from the oxer at **B**, taking one canter stride between **A-B**, or **B-A**. When your horse is settled in, you can then add a 2-foot vertical at **C** with a 9-foot (2.7m) placing pole behind **C**. At this point the gymnastic will be complete as shown below.

Approach **A** at the trot, jump the vertical, take one canter stride, jump the low-wide oxer, again take one canter stride and finish over the vertical at **C**. You can increase the difficulty by raising the verticals at **A** and **C** while maintaining the low-wide oxer as it was originally set. Thus, your horse must compress his stride to jump the first vertical, stretch his body out over the low-wide oxer at **B**, and finally recover his balance in order to rock back on his haunches and jump the vertical at **C**.

Once you are comfortably jumping the verticals at **A** and **C** (which are set at, or just below, the height of your competitive level) you can then start to spread the oxer—without changing its height. This is painstaking work, because each time you change the spread, you need to change the distance to the next vertical to re-establish that distance at 18 feet.

At some point, as the verticals get bigger, when jumping from **A** to **C** I move the last ground pole at **C** out from 9 to 10 feet (3m). (This relationship will change according to the horse and the height of the fence being jumped.) The important points are that you want your horse to drop his head and neck over the vertical, and to look where he is going to put his feet down behind the last fence. If your horse does not bend his back sufficiently yet in his arc over the obstacle, and lands beyond the ground pole, immediately move the ground pole away from the obstacle a couple

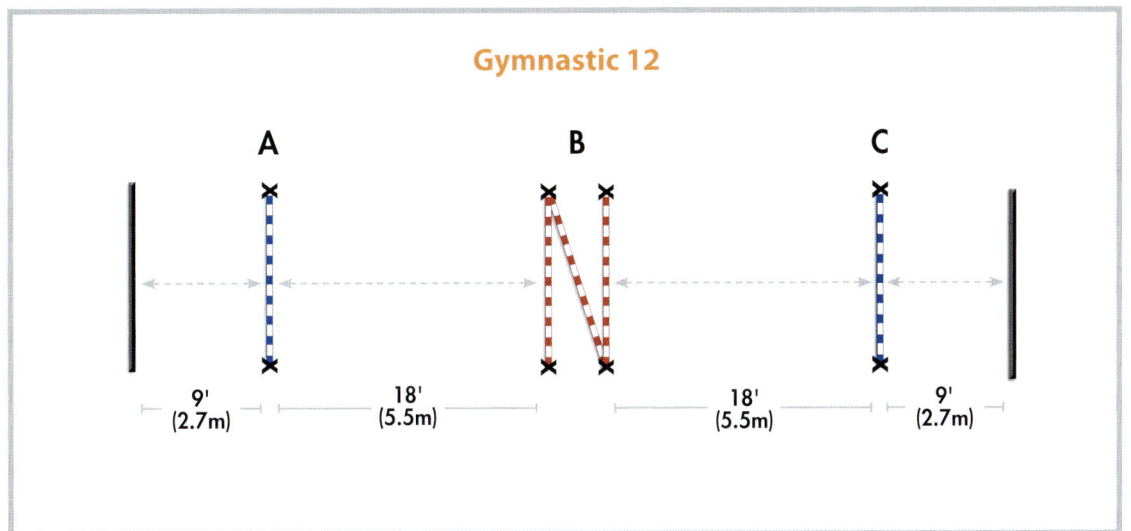

Gymnastic 12

GYMNASTIC 12 Alyssa Peterson's horse, Music Man, is on his toes as they approach Gymnastic 12 and has just started a canter stride over the placing pole. Alyssa has done a good job with her reins, lifting her hand the same amount that Music has lifted his head so as to maintain a straight line from her elbow to Music's mouth. She can tell he is keen, and she is supporting and controlling without restraining.

This pair has already had several repetitions through the gymnastic at lower heights, and successfully jumped verticals 6 inches higher at **A** and **C** with the oxer 6 inches lower. This photo sequence illustrates the opposite presentation, with the verticals lower but the oxer higher. When the oxer at **B** is raised, Music notices and reacts to the change. While his powerful gathering stride has tipped Alyssa slightly ahead of his motion, she has her legs applied at the girth and a straight line from her elbow to Music's mouth.

The image over **B** shows the horse's reaction when I start to change the shape or size of the obstacles. The diagonal rail over a low-wide oxer is a safety factor because it prevents your horse from thinking the low-wide oxer is a bounce. As I start to lower the verticals and raise the oxer, the same diagonal rail will cause many horses to lift their shoulders a bit more than usual. Because she could feel Music preparing for an extra-powerful effort at the oxer, Alyssa is too high above the saddle at the peak of the bascule.

Music is no fool. As he lands after the oxer, he is already assessing the final vertical. Realizing that it is not very high, he produces an effort at **C** that suits the size and shape of the fence. Gymnastic jumping teaches your horse to measure the obstacle carefully as he approaches it, and to think about what he is going to do when he gets there.

of feet. Once he relaxes, you can start to move the ground pole back to the correct distance—but do this gradually, so your horse does not feel claustrophobic about the landing distance.

Your horse may have a slight tendency to rush between **B** and **C**, but make a concerted effort to stay poised over his withers and jump the exercise on soft reins. Throughout these gymnastics, it is essential that you teach your horse to stay in balance without depending on contact with your reins. If he becomes more and more exuberant, you can place poles on the ground 9 feet (2.7m) in front of and 9 feet (2.7m) after the oxer at **B**. This will assist him in maintaining the regularity of his stride.

Gymnastic 13 (p. 65)

You and your horse first encountered bounces with Gymnastic 5, where he learned to jump and jump again without an intervening stride—and you learned to maintain your two-point and follow his motion by opening and closing your elbow. In this more advanced gymnastic, bounces are one of the ways in which we ask your horse for increased flexibility in his stride.

Gymnastic 13 is the reverse of Gymnastic 12. Previously, we asked your horse to compress his body, then expand, and then compress his body again. In this new gymnastic, we are going to expand his body first, then compress him during the double bounce, and then expand his body again out over the final low-wide oxer.

If you have enough rails and standards, it is a very good idea to construct Gymnastics 12 and 13 side by side. Then, if your horse becomes overly exuberant during Gymnastic 12, you have an alternative immediately at hand that teaches him to re-balance himself. The double bounce in the middle of Gymnastic 13 has a wonderfully compressing effect on the length of your horse's stride.

Start your warm-up as usual with the poles on the ground 9 feet (2.7m) apart and then build a 2-foot vertical at **A**. When your horse is com-

GYMNASTIC 13 is designed to teach your horse to expand and contract his body. The shape of the obstacles and the distance between them will determine the expansion and contraction. In the meantime, you should be an intelligent passenger on your horse; don't let him run out, don't let him refuse, don't kick (much) and don't pull. Let the gymnastic train your horse for you.

Edward Ewbank and Finn start the gymnastic correctly. Like most horses, Finn has jumped up, rather than across the low-wide oxer. Like most riders, Edward is too high out of the saddle. Despite these minor errors, they land in balance and are taking two strides to the double bounce in the center of the gymnastic.

Finn is too loose with his forelegs jumping into the double bounce. Hanging his forelegs can be a sign of Finn's inexperience, a sign of Edward leaning too far out of the saddle too soon—or both. Finn recognizes his error in the middle of the bounce and is much better with his forelegs over the next rail. Edward is balanced above Finn's center of gravity, although too high above his back. (The farther our center of gravity is from our horse's, the harder it is to stay in harmony.)

Leaving the double bounce, this pair is in balance and starting the first of the measured two strides to the final low-wide oxer. Finn is looking at the oxer, which leads me to think that his arc will be more across the oxer this time, rather than over-jumping it.

fortable jumping the vertical at the trot, turn fence **A** into a low-wide oxer 18 inches to 2 feet high, and 3 feet wide. Trot several times back and forth until your horse is relaxed. Then, 30 feet (9.1m) away from the low-wide oxer's back rail, add a bounce by building 2-foot verticals at **B** and **C**. Each time you add an obstacle to the gymnastic, approach from the "new" side first. Your horse will naturally concentrate on the new addition, and you want him to deal with it first, so that when he lands he is looking at obstacles he has already jumped successfully. Make sure your horse is confident approaching from **C** first, before approaching from **A**.

Once you are sure your horse understands, trot back and forth several times. For example, if you trot in over **A** your horse should land at the canter, take two regular strides and jump the bounce at **B** (and later at **C**). Again, trot both ways several times. When you are sure your horse understands both the low-wide oxer to the single-bounce, and the single-bounce sequences, you can add the next vertical at **D**, the same height as **B** and **C**. Repeat the exercise, approaching first towards the double-bounce, followed in

Advanced Jumping

two strides by the low-wide oxer, and then back the other way.

If this is going well, you can add the final oxer at **E**, the same height and spread as the oxer at **A**, with a 9-foot placing pole behind **E**. Although you can now approach the entire exercise at the trot from either direction, start by approaching the new low-wide oxer at **E**.

There are two ways to increase the difficulty of this gymnastic. First, you can raise the verticals at **B, C** and **D**, in 3-inch increments, which will cause your horse to compress his body a great deal more. Once he is comfortable with this change, you can spread the oxers at **A** and **E**. Remember to move the outside rail of the oxers to change the spread, and to re-measure the 9-foot (2.7m) distance to the ground pole in both directions. By the time you have done all the repetitions that comprise the complete gymnastic, you should only go through the whole series a maximum of twice each day. That will be enough jumping for your horse, especially if it is the first time he has done this gymnastic exercise.

Gymnastic 13

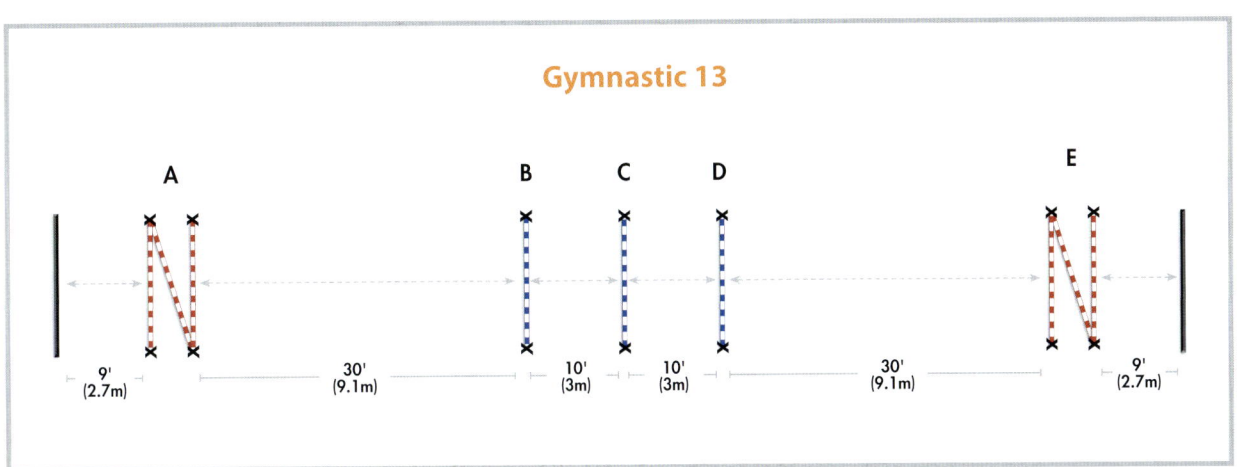

MODERN GYMNASTICS 65

GYMNASTIC 14A is very sophisticated and is not suitable for horses working over gymnastics for the first time. At the same time, it is quite useful for horses that tend to gain speed as they proceed through a combination or a related line of obstacles. Claire Kelley's Orion XII is the sort of horse that needs this gymnastic: He is quite experienced, but on his forehand and too aggressive at the end of his lines.

Claire and Orion start well over the first vertical leading into the initial bounce, but we can see the "on the forehand" part of his style by looking at his technique over the first three bounce rails. Throughout the double bounce his forearms are low. I like to see the horse's forearms above the horizontal, with his knees forming a three-sided box at the peak of his bascule. Claire is in a good position over all three verticals. The angle of her upper body to the ground is consistent, although I would like to see her in a light three-point in the landing stride. One stride later, Claire has regained her balance; she is admirably placed and waiting for Orion to jump the hogsback.

In the next image, I think Orion's effort over the hogsback has taken Claire by surprise and she is slightly behind the motion at the peak of the bascule. She has compensated for this by extending her elbows. From the look on Orion's face, he could not care less.

I like hogsbacks because they conform exactly to the shape of the perfect bascule. They produce round, "lofty" efforts—exactly what we want.

Gymnastic 14 (p. 68)

This is one of my favorite gymnastics for teaching horses not to rush. Begin Gymnastic 14 as usual with two poles on the ground 9 feet (2.7m) apart. Continue by building a 2-foot vertical, then trot back and forth over these elements to warm your horse up.

At this stage of your horse's training he should be quite businesslike in his approach, and you can proceed to build the remaining obstacles in Gymnastic 14 without too many repetitions. First, trot back and forth over a single bounce at **A** and **B**, then build and ride back and forth over a double bounce, approaching at the trot towards **C, B** and then **A** (remember, new obstacle first.) Once you are successful, come back the other way, **A** to **B** to **C**. When your horse is relaxed in this exercise you can then build a "hogsback" at **D**, 28 feet (8.5m) from **C**. (A hogsback is an obstacle with a very low rail first, a higher middle rail, and a final rail the same height as the first rail. See photo above.)

The overall spread of the hogsback should be about 3-foot-6, with the middle rail at from 2-foot-6 to 3 feet. I like to keep the first and last rails of the hog's back quite low, raising only the middle rail to increase its difficulty. Unless the horse is experienced, I will usually have the rider

Advanced Jumping

approach at a slight angle to jump the hogsback as a single obstacle first, before I ask the horse to deal with it in the gymnastic sequence. Once your horse understands the hogsback, approach at the trot from **A** through to **D**, landing at the canter after the double bounce, taking two strides and jumping the hogsback at **D**.

The distance between **C** and **D** is designed to place your horse's front feet quite close to the front rail of the hogsback. At first this might be a slightly uncomfortable sensation for you both, but you should get used to it; this is the correct place to take off in front of fences of this shape.

When you are comfortable jumping the double bounce, landing, taking two strides and jumping out over the hogsback, you should then approach the hogsback at **D** at the canter, jump it, land and take two strides coming out in the other direction over the double bounce.

Following this, you can build the second set of bounce rails at **E, F** and **G**, using the same dimensions as at **C, B** and **A**. Your horse can now trot in both directions over this exercise. Gradually you should raise the middle rail of the hogsback until your horse is jumping it at least 3 inches higher than his competitive level.

Younger horses seem to understand this

GYMNASTIC 14B As we watch him over the double bounce that follows the hogsback, it is obvious why I said this is a good gymnastic for Orion. Horses that have to deal with another double bounce at the end of a line of fences soon learn to keep their shoulders in front of them, instead of rushing through the line of jumps. Orion will be a more mature horse the next time he does this gymnastic.

Looking at the second series of images gives me the feeling that Orion has made a serious adjustment at the last instant. He has "popped up" over the first vertical of this next double bounce, but has left his forelegs low as he does so. This can produce a jolting sensation to the rider, and the motion has pushed Claire out of the saddle too much.

The excellence of Claire's lower-leg position saves the day for her, although her shoulders have gotten too far out in front of her knees and she is in a precarious situation. Orion will make the same sort of shape over the last vertical coming out of the bounce, and Claire's lower-leg position enables her to extricate herself from a potentially dangerous situation.

When I have horses that are too aggressive at the end of their gymnastics or in-and-outs, I will repeat this gymnastic several times, until I can tell that the horse is recovering his own balance after the hogsback.

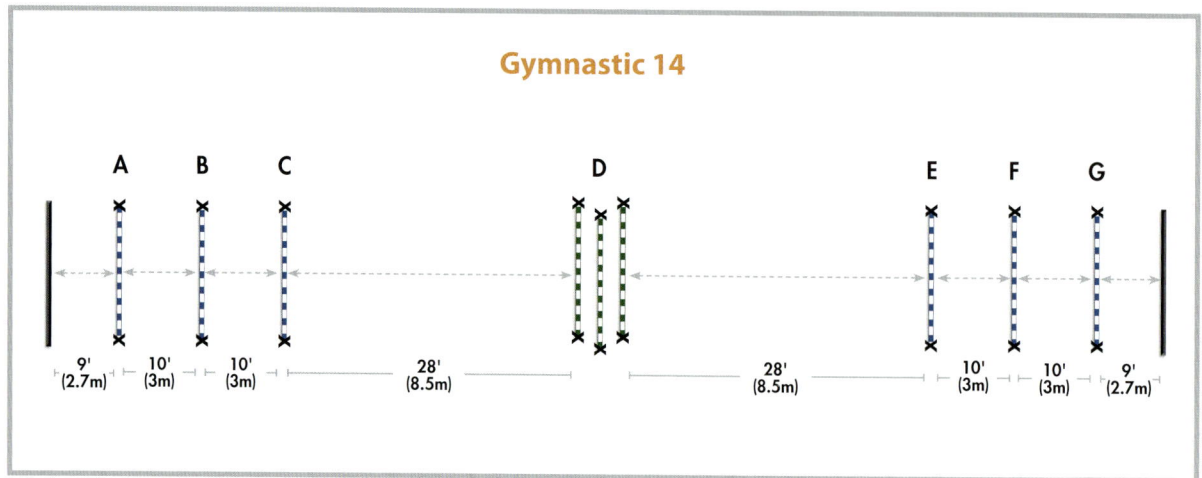

exercise well enough, but for them I usually move the outside rails of the hogsback 6 inches closer to the middle rail, thus increasing the distance slightly between the hogsback and the bounces and also decreasing the spread of the hogsback. Once your horse has seen this exercise a couple of times, he should be able to jump a hogsback with a spread of 5 feet (1.5m) and a height at center rail of 3-foot-6 (1.06m) quite easily.

If your horse becomes a bit exuberant after jumping a larger hogsback, you can raise the double bounce rails at **A-B-C** and **E-F-G** in 3-inch increments as a deterrent. Just as in Gymnastic 13, allow your horse to learn from the exercise, rather than learning to listen to you. Try to teach him to keep his own balance rather than relying on your grip on the reins. Horses can rush through a single bounce and jump "over their shoulders" (on their forehand). However, they will very quickly learn not to overcommit their body when jumping a double bounce; they have to keep their center of balance behind their shoulder in order to negotiate the exercise comfortably.

6
Cross-Country Gymnastics

Cross-country gymnastics have the same benefit to your horse as regular show-jumping gymnastics and should be done with the same ideas in mind. Your horse should maintain his balance and regularity, and you should be poised over his center of gravity and riding with soft reins throughout these exercises. Even if your horse is going to be a show jumper, some work up and down slopes can be very beneficial to him, as it teaches him to keep his balance going downhill and to push with his hocks going uphill—and balance and energy are what the jumping game is all about.

Gymnastic 15 (p. 70)

Gymnastic 15 is important because it is the first time you will introduce your horse to jumping up and down slopes. Until now, all your work should have been on level ground. Working on sloping ground is an essential skill for horses such as eventers and foxhunters that perform on uneven—rising or falling—ground. Given enough education and experience, horses can deal with very steep terrain, even when it includes difficult obstacles. However, just as with most things involving horses, you must take the time and teach your horse how to deal with the problems posed by changes in terrain. As you will see, the exercises in this section are designed to produce the same rhythm and balance that we have been seeking in the gymnastics you rode on level ground in previous sections.

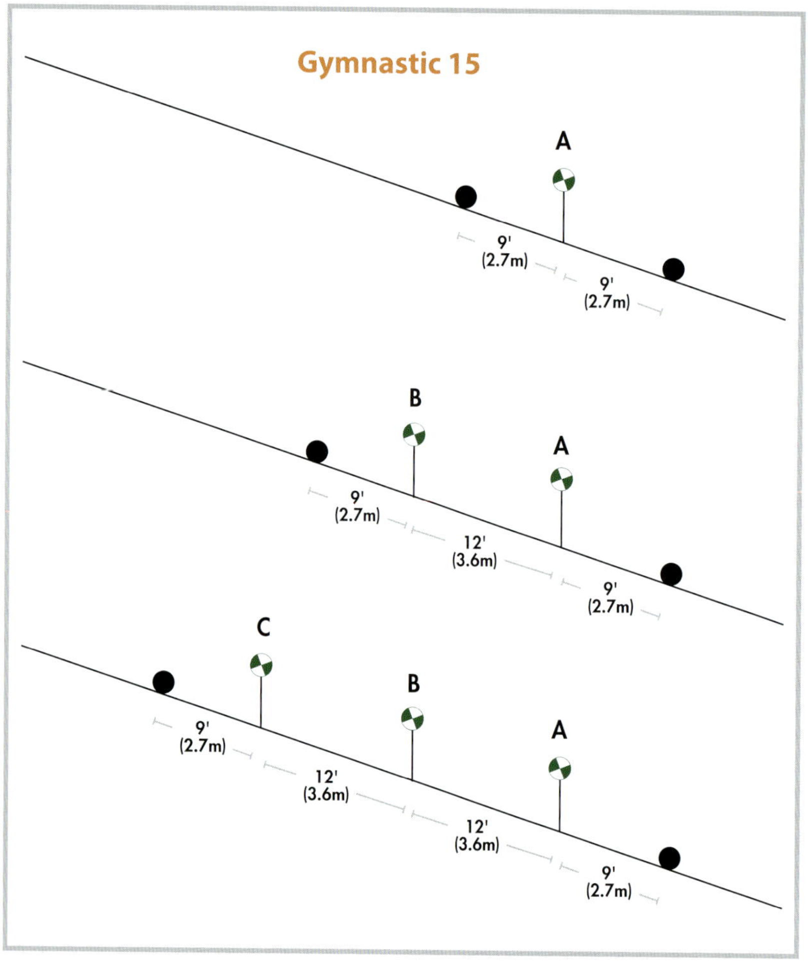

Begin your cross-country gymnastic work on a very mild slope. Put two poles on the ground 9 feet (2.7m) apart, and then trot uphill and downhill over them. Be aware of the influence of the terrain on your and your horse's balance. For example, when you are trotting uphill your weight must be even more determinedly in your heels, and the forward inclination at your waist should be greater; although soft and light in the contact, your reins should be slightly shorter, as a reminder to keep your balance up over your horse's shoulders.

On the other hand, when you are trotting and (later) cantering downhill over the rails on the slope, your reins should be a bit longer, your lower leg should be slightly in front of the girth and the angle at your hip should be a bit more open to assist you in keeping your center of gravity behind your horse's shoulders. Going either uphill or down, your stirrup leathers should remain vertical. (Remember, vertical and perpendicular are not the same thing … vertical is an absolute concept, while perpendicular is relative.)

Once you feel comfortable trotting and cantering over the rails on the ground, build a 2-foot vertical at **A**, as shown in the diagram of Gymnastic 15 at left, with a 9-foot (2.7m) placing pole before and after the fence. Practice back and forth over this small obstacle at both trot and canter until you are comfortable jumping up- and downhill. Remember that when jumping uphill, you should land after the obstacle with the

Gymnastic 15

weight very much in your knees and ankles and your seat higher out of the saddle than usual. It is easy to fall behind the motion jumping uphill, just as it is easy to topple in front of the motion jumping downhill. Both mistakes interfere with your horse's balance, so work hard to prevent them from happening.

Before jumping uphill, shorten your reins to a few inches less than your normal length. This will help lead your upper body up your horse's neck. In addition, as your horse jumps the 2-foot rail at **A** make sure you press your heels down and slightly back. If you make a mistake jumping uphill, it should be that your lower leg is slightly behind the vertical. Between your hands being farther up the neck and your lower leg slightly behind, you will have a tendency to land after an uphill jump well placed over your horse's withers, which is exactly where you should be in this situation.

When jumping downhill, reverse my sugges-

GYMNASTIC 15A Sharon White and Don Sheffield are handling this gymnastic well. "Shu" obviously understands the question; at the peak of his bascule he has his eyes on the landing after each jump, is obviously mobile with his shoulders and is staying straight up the hill. From the engagement of his haunches, you can see the extra effort that jumping uphill requires.

Jumping uphill also requires us to make adjustments in our position. In both photos, Sharon has driven her heel down. This enables her to stay with the motion and to keep her shoulders in advance of her knees. Her position over both verticals is very similar, with her back at the same angle to the ground over both elements. Sharon has responded to Shu's extra effort over the second vertical by exaggerating her forward motion. This ensures that she will not get left behind. Once I was happy that Shu understood the uphill bounce, I added a third vertical and created a double-bounce. You can see that illustrated in the next photo, where I ask Sharon and Shu to jump a downhill double-bounce.

GYMNASTIC 15B The expression on Shu's face tells us that he is thinking hard about the double-bounce. You can see that he is making an extra effort to land with his front feet out in front of his shoulders. This helps him keep his balance as he jumps downhill. Once horses understand this gymnastic, they keep their head and neck a little high to keep their front feet in front of their body. Compare the use of Shu's head and neck while jumping the uphill bounce in the previous photo with this one, where he obviously does not complete his bascule.

Jumping downhill requires that we adjust our position to compensate for the downhill landing. You can see that Sharon has her seat very close to her saddle and she has lengthened her reins, so that she can follow Shu's motion without toppling over. Her legs are secure at the girth and her ankles are accepting the shock of landing. Except for a slight lean at the third vertical, Sharon's upper body stays at exactly the same angle throughout the gymnastic.

tions above; that is, as you make a downhill approach to the obstacle at **A** in Exercise 15, I now want you to open your hip angle, so that you are more erect than a moment ago when you were jumping uphill. Place your lower leg slightly in front of you and slip your reins a few inches, to allow for the fact that your horse's neck will be slightly lower and farther away than if he were on the flat. As you jump the obstacle at **A**, do not follow your horse's effort with your upper body; rather, think that you are going to push the points of your hips forward. Sometimes I tell students to "stand up" rather than "bend over" as their horse jumps downhill. My intention is that you land above vertical stirrup leathers and take the shock of landing in your knees and ankles. You should learn not to throw away the reins when you jump a drop, but rather allow the horse to "slip" the reins through your fingers and then quickly and smoothly regain the reins. The best way to gather your reins quickly is illustrated by the photos on page 77.

When you are comfortable trotting and cantering up- and downhill, you can place another 2-foot (0.6m) vertical—shown in the diagram as **B**—12 feet (3.6m) away from the first with a 9-foot (2.7m) placing pole behind it. Notice that I have used a 12-foot (3.6m) distance in the bounce on sloping cross-country terrain, while I used a 10-foot (3m) distance in the bounces on flat terrain. This is because when your horse is jumping downhill, he will need a little more room to land than on the flat; when jumping uphill, on the other hand, the same distance will be slightly long. This is a good thing, as it encourages your horse to push his body forward and encourages you to ride with your lower legs, not with your reins. In addition, you now have an exercise that you can jump in both directions.

After you have practiced over the single bounce at **A** and **B**, add a third 2-foot rail at **C**, as shown in the diagram, to create a double bounce.

Once your horse is comfortable trotting and cantering straight uphill and straight downhill over the double bounce, vary your work by approaching on a curve. For example, canter on the left lead turning left-handed uphill to the double bounce, jump the exercise and pull up going up the slope. Then turn and come back downhill on the right lead, practicing turning across and down the slope into the double bounce exercise. Once your horse shows that he understands the exercise, practice on both leads uphill and downhill. I usually turn after the last rail in the opposite direction than that from which I approached. Your horse should be equally balanced on both leads in this gymnastic. In addition, you should gradually decrease the amount of time he has to evaluate the gymnastic in the approach. He needs to become accustomed to meeting fences and thinking about them quickly, even as he deals with the balance problems posed by changing terrain. Although the obstacles are set at 2 feet to start, you can certainly raise them as your horse matures. However, due to the compressed striding that a bounce requires, you should raise the rails very gradually. As a rule of thumb, I consider raising the bounce rails 3 inches to be the equivalent (in difficulty) of raising a normal obstacle 6 inches.

Gymnastic 16 (p. 74)

Horses find banks to be very natural, and they take to them easily. I think this is because jumping a bank separates the jumping effort into two parts. When your horse jumps up a bank, he needs to push his body high enough to reach the next step, but there is no shock of landing. When he trots or canters across the bank and steps down, he must deal only with the landing phase, without having first pushed his body up. By separating the jumping effort into two parts, your horse can relax and focus on each aspect of his effort. Later on, you will notice that he is better when jumping normal obstacles.

For this gymnastic you will need a small permanent bank. In order to teach the horse about banks in the simplest possible manner, I prefer to begin with square banks on level ground. The height of the bank should be approximately 2 feet (20cm). I prefer that the bank be flat across the top, as later on I can create a jump here with portable rails. This allows me to regulate the difficulty according to the reaction of the horse to each particular situation.

Trot and canter both ways up and down the bank. Review my comments regarding the placement of your body above your horse when jumping up- and downhill. The motion of jumping up and down the bank is merely an exaggerated form of the sensations you have already felt jumping up and down a slope during Gymnastic 15.

Once your horse is comfortable trotting and cantering up and down the bank, place two poles on the ground 9 feet (2.7m) apart on the top level of the bank as shown in the diagram below. The pole closest to the edge of the bank should be 18 feet (5.5m) from the drop. Trot from the rails to the drop first so that your horse looks at the change in the exercise, and then steps down over a bank he has already jumped. The standards you will use for obstacles **A** and **B** should be in position, but without rails. This allows your horse to see where the standards are and reminds you to proceed in a straight line both riding towards and going away from the obstacle.

You should trot and, later on, canter both ways over the bank several times before you start to add obstacles. When stepping up the bank, make sure you land well forward, poised over vertical stirrup leathers and with your reins correctly adjusted. (You should only slip your reins

when jumping down, not when jumping on the level or jumping up.) As your horse's front feet touch the next level, you should have quite a bit of space between your seat bones and the saddle. As he brings his hindquarters up to the next level, you should have the feeling that he has brought his back up to meet your seat bones, rather than that you are falling back to touch the saddle. In

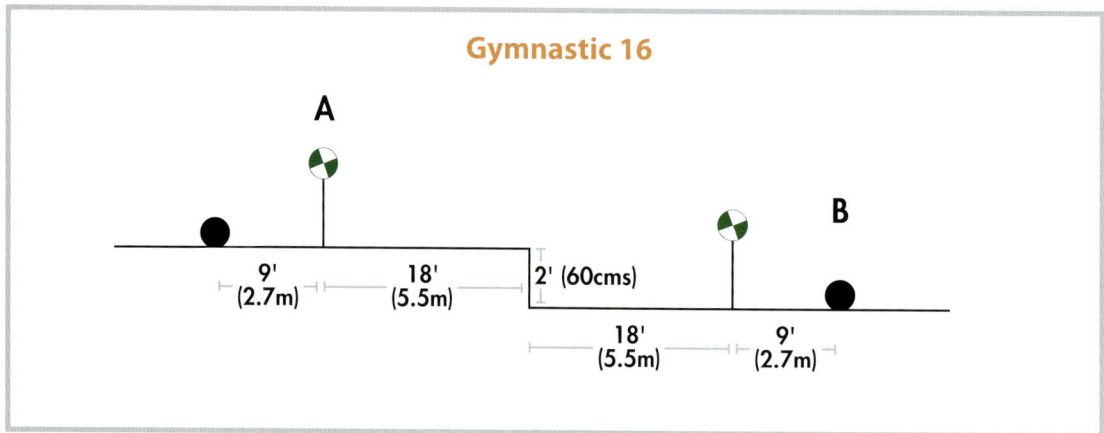

GYMNASTIC 16 This series of photos was taken after Clare Green and Balustrade had been carefully introduced to the bank first with no ground poles, then a ground pole and a vertical, and so on, as described in the text. Although "Bailey" is quite green, she is willing, and the jumps are low enough that she is not overfaced. I like the expression on her face; she is focused and thinking about her next move, which is exactly what you want gymnastics to teach your horse.

Ordinarily, I want the reins loose for low gymnastics. However, Clare needs a little extra contact to help give her young horse confidence, and she has it about right in this series. Clare is in exactly the right place over the first vertical. The really interesting moment is Clare's position as Bailey makes a nice effort up the bank. Horses cannot do a "chin-up" to pull themselves up to the next level. They must jump their own height above the bank, and land with their knees almost locked. Riders are quite often left behind jumping up banks, because they do not understand this mechanism.

As they jump up onto the bank, Clare's stirrup leather is still vertical, which allows her to follow Bailey's motion correctly. You can tell from their poise and confidence in the final photo that they will jump the last vertical easily.

I often school young horses up and down small banks, many times without any rails or logs involved. When horses jump up a bank, they do not have to worry about their landing. Conversely, when they jump down, they need only drop off the top and can concentrate completely on their landing. Because we separate the bascule into two parts, our horse can study the parts of the whole and learn to jump more easily.

the first complete stride on top of the bank you should be in a light three-point position, with your reins adjusted correctly.

When your horse understands how to jump up and down the bank, you can place a 2-foot vertical at **A** as shown in the diagram on page 74. Trot from the 9-foot (2.7m) placing pole to **A**, land, take one stride, and allow your horse to step down and canter out through the open standards at **B**. (Remember, if the terrain is level you should be in a normal show-jumping position when your horse jumps the obstacle at **A**.)

When he lands from **A** and takes his stride before jumping down the bank, you should still remain in a normal show-jumping position.

As your horse steps down off the bank, you should have the sensation that you are pushing the points of your hips forward and down. Soften your fingers so that your horse can stretch his head and neck down into the landing after the bank. Do not take an exaggerated position backward with your head and neck; this will cause you to lift your hands up and back, pulling on your horse's mouth and interfering with the use of his head and neck. Just as when jumping up the bank, make sure you land with vertical stirrup leathers.

When you slip the reins to follow your horse's mouth down the drop, re-establish the correct length of rein and contact as soon as you can, using the technique illustrated on the facing page: As you canter away from the bank, lift your reins with one hand and slide them through the fingers of your other hand, thus re-establishing a normal length. This will not come naturally to you at first and it is something that you should practice when you are walking around the field to take a break between gymnastics.

It is usually easier on your horse to trot at **A**, then jump down the bank. When jumping up the bank, approach at the canter, jump the bank, take one stride and jump the vertical at **A**.

Once your horse is comfortable with this, you can add another 2-foot vertical at **B** with a placing pole 9 feet from **B** on the side opposite the bank. Approach at the canter from **B** towards the bank so that the new part of the gymnastic is the first part your horse sees. I find that if you first approach from the other direction (**A** to **B**), the less-experienced horse will often make a mistake at **A**, even though he has just jumped it successfully in both directions. He will lose his concentration at **A** due to looking ahead at the new element at **B**. If you approach from the direction of **B**, your horse will usually remain focused and willing, even though we have increased the difficulty.

After your horse has jumped successfully—landing over **B**, taking a stride, jumping up the bank, taking another single stride, jumping again and landing after **A** in a poised and balanced fashion—you are ready to come back the other way around, from **A** down to **B**. This is a tricky moment; you will have the sensation as you jump down the bank that **B** is too close, but do not panic and pull back on the reins in an attempt to shorten your horse's stride. As with so many things in riding, this action will create the condition that you were trying to prevent. When you pull back on the reins, you invert your horse's back. This will cause him to jump farther off the bank, land too close to **B** and make an awkward effort at the next obstacle—or indeed, knock it down.

Your actions should instead be: Approach at the trot and jump **A**, landing with your reins organized, because it is too early to let your reins get long. As your horse steps to the end of his stride before jumping down the bank, let the reins soften so that he can lower his head and neck. Your thinking should not be that you want to pull your horse's stride away from the takeoff point before **B**, but rather that after **A** you want him to step down quietly, close to the base of the bank.

Obviously, the closer you land behind the bank, the more room your horse will have to fit in his stride and the more comfortable your effort will be jumping out over **B**. If your horse is green and "launches" off the bank, you can usually solve this problem by putting a placing pole halfway (9 feet, or 2.7m) between the bank and the vertical at **B**.

Practice this exercise a great deal if you are a cross-country rider, because it simulates many of the situations that you will find yourself in when going across country.

If your horse has become adept jumping from **A** to **B** and **B** to **A**, you can start to alter the distances. For example, you can move **A** in until it is 10 feet (3m) from the lip of the bank, which will cause your horse to land over **A**, bounce down the bank and take a stride to **B**. Alternatively, when jumping back from **B** to **A** your horse will jump **B**, take one stride, step up on the bank and bounce out over the rail at **A**.

I usually place rails on the ground first when I am doing new exercises, to show the horse where the obstacle will be the next time through. Rehearse your horse over the new distances using rails on the ground, then keep the obstacles small at first, to make sure he understands the gymnastic. Once he understands

Gathering Reins

At the halt, Loreen Kay practices slipping and recovering her reins. In this image, her left hand is just about to reach in front of her right hand. You should practice this motion until you can recover your reins with either hand. Start this motion with both hands close together, so that you know where your reins are without having to look down for them.

Recovering your reins after a drop is like drawing a bow and arrow. While one hand lifts up and back towards the point of your shoulder, your other hand slides up the reins, making sure it stays above the crest of the mane, so as not to get tangled in the mane. Move your forward hand to his ears, not to his neck. You can see my hand in the photo, adjusting Loreen's forward hand a little higher next time. At this point, drop the knot with the hand that went to your shoulder and take the rein again with that hand. You are ready to gallop to the next fence with your reins adjusted.

the questions asked, the height and spread will be no problem.

The variation in gymnastic exercises that you can set up using portable rails around banks is limited only by your imagination and the level of training that you wish to achieve with your horse. If you first rehearse him over rails on the ground, you will be surprised at the complexity of the exercise you can build once he understands the nature of the problem. For example, you can teach your horse to jump narrow fences, corners and bounces both before and after the bank. By changing the location of the obstacles, you can teach your horse to turn on landing after having jumped up the bank and to jump **A** on an angle—or land and jump on a curve three strides going downhill at **B**. You can create a "distances" gymnastic quite similar to Gymnastic 8 on page 50, which can be jumped in both directions.

The variation in gymnastic exercises that you can set up using portable rails around banks is limited only by your imagination and the level of training you wish to achieve with your horse.

All of these gymnastics will teach your horse to be flexible, land in balance and wait for you to determine the direction and the striding.

As the height of the obstacles at **A** and **B** increases, you may need to increase the distance between the bank and **B**. This is quite acceptable. Just watch your horse's reactions carefully and adjust the distance accordingly. The distances given between **A** and **B** work well when the bank is on level ground. However, if the bank is on a slope or if there is a permanent log at the top of the bank, this may change the nature of the exercise; again, you will need to adjust the distances between the portable elements accordingly. If you do not have expert supervision and start having uncomfortable fences, my suggestion is to look at the hoofprints, and then adjust the distances to suit your horse. When you start using these gymnastics, a 17-hand, 5-year-old Thoroughbred may need more room between obstacles in order to produce comfortable, rhythmical jumping efforts, while a small horse with a choppy stride may need for you to make the distances much shorter. My advice is to make these exercises comfortable for your horse's individual stride first; later on, you can train him to take a 12-foot stride between obstacles.

Gymnastic 17 (p. 79)

Ditches are a necessary part of your horse's education, especially if you are going to foxhunt or event him. While every event horse should jump ditches well, many horses need a careful introduction in order to make sure they are confident about jumping them. A green horse can be trained to jump ditches easily, but during his first few exposures to jumping a ditch, make sure to have an experienced and trustworthy older horse who can give your novice a lead if necessary.

Before jumping a formal ditch, find a gentle swale in a field somewhere and take three rustic rails to that location. Put two of the rails down in the middle of the swale on the ground approximately 24 inches (60cm) apart, with the third rail laid diagonally across them. Then trot back and forth over this simulated ditch, gradually increasing the spread to 3 feet (90cm).

If you can find a swale next to a very small revetted ditch, about 2 feet wide and not too deep ("revetted" means that either one or both sides of the ditch have been reinforced), this is even better; the horse seems to transfer his attention from one to the other without too much trouble. By all means use a lead, and approach at the canter at first. When jumping the simulated ditch, be quite vigorous. If your horse stops at the simulated ditch despite following another horse, you should make him walk over the rails on the ground, even if you have to be very aggressive with your aids. Repeat the simulated ditch in the same direction until your horse is calm and confident. Then have him repeat the process in the opposite direction, again following another horse at first, and then by himself.

Ditches are really a question of obedience rather than of jumping ability, and you should treat them as such. A good test of your horse's confidence over the simulated ditch is to count out loud the rhythm of both the approach and the departure. If you can approach, jump the simulated ditch, and depart at the same speed and with the same rhythm, then you can be fairly certain that your horse is ready to progress to the next level of difficulty.

Before you move to the next series, place a pair of standards on each side of the ditch as shown in the illustration on this page. Next, take the three rustic poles that you used to create the simulated ditch, and place one on each side of the small revetted ditch, with the third pole diagonally across the ditch as before with the simulated ditch. Repeat the same process: have a more experienced horse give yours a lead back and forth over the small revetted ditch. Then canter your horse back and forth over the ditch on his own until you are positive he is confident. Once you are sure he understands, gradually take the three poles away—the diagonal pole first, then one back rail and finally the front, so that he jumps the ditch without the visual aids. (If the ditch is only revetted on one side, leave a rustic pole on the other side so that you can jump it both directions.) His calmness will be satisfactory if he can approach the revetted ditch without a lead, jump and depart, all in the same rhythm.

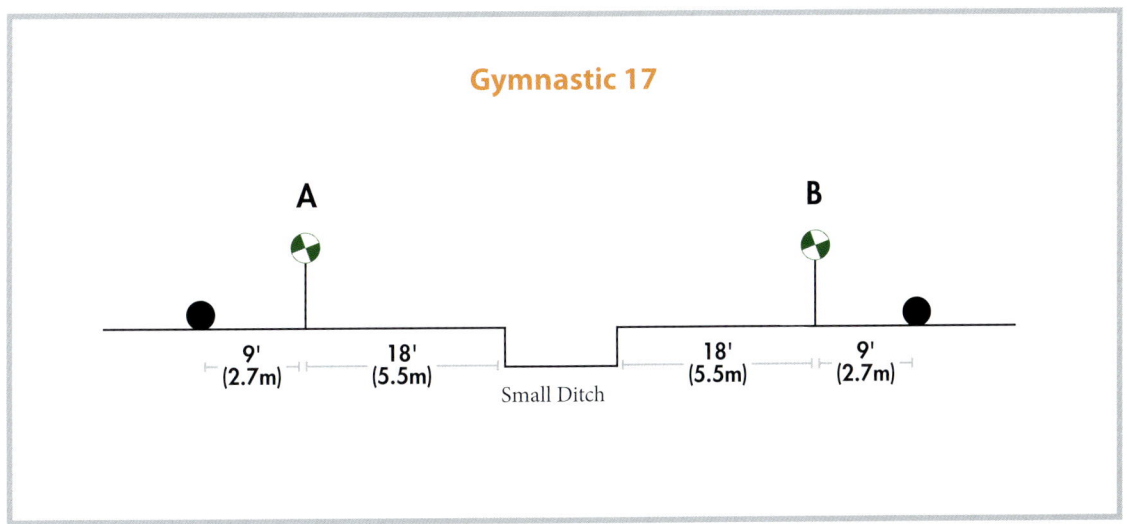

Now put a pole on the ground between two standards, 18 feet (5.5m) from the ditch. Place another ground pole 9 feet (2.7m) from the first pole—27 feet (8.2m) from the ditch—and canter back and forth over this exercise. Once your horse is confident about the addition of two poles to the ditch, you can build a 2-foot vertical at **A**. Trot in over the ground pole, jump the small vertical and make sure your horse takes one stride before jumping the ditch. Then turn around, canter back through the open standards where you will place **B** in a moment, jump the ditch, land, take one stride and jump out over **A** in the opposite direction. When your horse has shown—by jumping calmly through in both directions—that he understands the question, you can build a 2-foot vertical at **B**, again with a 9-foot (2.7m) placing rail behind it. Trot from **B** to **A** first. (As before, whenever I change a green horse's environment, I try to confront him with the new part first, followed by obstacles he is already comfortable with. Once he has gone through from **B** to **A**, he will be much more willing to return from **A** to **B**.)

This gymnastic simulates a coffin, a normal question on cross-country courses at Training level and above. Again, the difficulty can be increased by increasing the height of the fences at **A** and **B**. I usually avoid raising the rail more than 3 inches at a time. As your horse gains confidence, you can raise the obstacles at **A** and **B** until they are quite respectable. My Preliminary event horses trot this exercise at 3-foot-6 (1.06m), over a ditch that is probably 3 feet (90cm) in width.

Once your horse is confirmed in understanding a basic coffin type of question, the same remarks as for Gymnastic 16 apply: the variations of this theme are endless and bounded only by your ingenuity. For example, more experienced horses should be able to jump a vertical 10 feet (3m) from the edge of the ditch and bounce over the ditch. Extremely experienced horses should be able to bounce, land and bounce again. The distance between **A** and **B** should be 10 feet (3m) on either side of the ditch. As usual, introduce this question by using ground poles at first, then 2-foot verticals. Your horse should be quite experienced before you raise the bounce rails much past 2 feet.

Further variations are jumping on an angle across the ditch to rails before and after, and/or jumping a narrow obstacle constructed over the ditch. Upper-level horses should practice narrow bounces, as this sort of fence is becoming increasingly popular at the Intermediate and Advanced levels of eventing.

GYMNASTIC 17 When you train horses using gymnastics, you always proceed from the simple to the more complex. When Clare Green and Balustrade started over the "ditch," it had no ground poles or verticals. I put "ditch" in quotes because I have used three rustic rails around a telephone pole buried in the ground to create the ditch in this gymnastic. In effect, I have built another low-wide oxer such as those your horse has already jumped in the arena.

To prepare for this series of photos, Clare and "Bailey" trotted back and forth over the ditch until Bailey relaxed and realized that small ditches are no big deal. Once the horse understands the basic problem, you can start to make the gymnastic more complex.

I like for riders to be closer to the saddle than Clare shows us over the vertical (on page 80, above left), especially if their horses are "ditchy" or sticky about ditches. Bailey has landed over the ditch quite close to the back rail. This is a sign she understands the problem, is not worried and can now safely be presented more complex combinations involving ditches. The photo over the ditch is interesting. If Clare and Bailey were cantering over level ground instead of jumping a small ditch, they would be in the same position.

One of the many benefits of gymnastics is that you can practice your position while you are educating your horse. Your two-point is the correct position for galloping, jumping and also the "up" phase of the posting trot. Although she is higher out of the saddle than she ideally should be, Clare's position is basically correct because the angle of her upper body to the ground does not change.

Gymnastic 18 (below)

Water is a part of going cross country, and it is important that your foxhunter or event horse is comfortable with water. They should jump into water, jump water-to-water, and jump out of water, all with confidence.

Introduce your horse to water with the same care that you used in teaching him to jump ditches. If you give him a bad experience in his formative stages, you will have a hard time with him later in his career, when fences of this nature become more difficult. Horses that will be show jumpers, however, should not undertake this gymnastic, because you do not ever want a show jumper to think it is permissible to step into water. For the same reason, you will not find water jumps in the show-jumping phase of an event these days; it is unfair to ask a horse to jump over water in the stadium phase after asking him to jump into water during cross country.

For schooling, I prefer a water jump that has at least one side that allows the horse to walk in and out without a jumping effort. It is absolutely essential that the water is shallow (6-9 inches) and that the footing is level and

firm underneath the surface. Jumping into water is a great test of your horse's courage and his confidence in you; these are traits that you must treasure and protect.

To begin, walk your horse through the water following a more experienced horse, then follow the lead horse through at a trot. Once your horse is relaxed and clearly understands the question, then walk and trot through the water without a

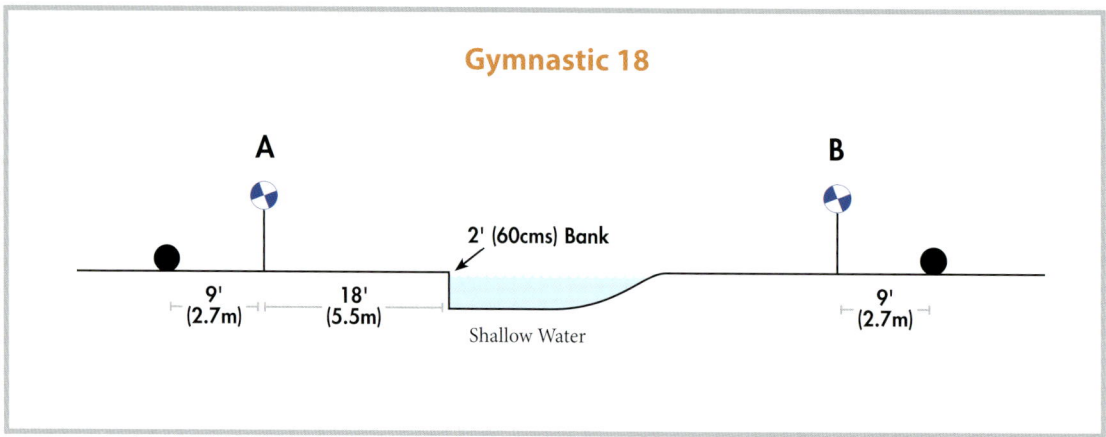

lead. If he is willing and confident, you can then canter back and forth. Your horse's confidence is your main concern during this lesson, because that will be the main question posed by water jumps throughout his competitive career.

Your horse will jump more willingly from the water back to dry ground than he will from dry ground down into the water, so it is better to rehearse in this direction first. Make sure that he trots and canters willingly down the slope into the water towards the bank and out onto dry land before attempting to jump from the bank down into the water. It is common for green horses to misjudge the bank when jumping out of water. For this reason, in the first few attempts at jumping up the bank out of water, I always have the rider hold the mane, so that whatever sort of awkward leap ensues, the rider is able to stay with the horse up to dry land. If the horse jumps awkwardly and the rider is left behind, it shakes the horse's confidence and he will remain

GYMNASTIC 18 Make sure your horse is very confident over Gymnastic 16 before attempting this gymnastic. Although the questions posed by the bank and rails in 18 are the same as those in 16, the addition of water complicates things. Clare Green and Balustrade have approached well, but "Bailey" shows her inexperience over the vertical. Her knees are a bit low, and her expression is somewhat doubtful.

I love the image between the vertical and the bank. Clare has applied a strong leg, yet has softened her hands and arms, giving Bailey a clear signal to go forward. The result is a brave leap into water from a green horse. Clare follows this mildly extravagant effort correctly by staying soft with her arms and using a slight slipping of her reins.

Remember to follow your horse's mouth with your elbows and shoulders, rather than with your hip angle. Notice how consistent Clare's body angle is to the ground. This is a sign of balance and sound fundamentals in the rider. Although Bailey is green, after several repetitions she went back and forth through this gymnastic willingly.

timid and inaccurate about jumping out of water for quite a while. It is better to avoid the mistake than to have to fix it.

Do not add further obstacles until you are convinced that your horse is confident about the question being asked and that he is enjoying his experience. Your rule of thumb should always be that you are on the right track if you can approach, jump, land and depart—all at the same speed.

Having made sure your horse is confident about jumping a small bank in and out of water, you can now proceed as you did in Gymnastic 16 for the dry bank (page 74).

Your horse will jump more willingly from the water back to dry ground than he will from dry ground down into the water, so it is better to rehearse in this direction first.

Put a rail on the ground 18 feet (5.5.m) away from the lip of the water obstacle's bank and a placing pole 9 feet (2.7m) before that. Trot in over the placing pole, jump down the bank and continue through the water and back out to dry land. Do this first at the trot, and then at the canter. I do not mind if your horse breaks back from canter to trot as he is going through this exercise, but it tells me he is not quite balanced and confident enough yet to increase the difficulty. Once he canters quietly through in both directions, raise the rail at **A** to 2 feet (60cm) and continue.

Afterwards, you can turn around and canter back, jumping from the water back up to dry land and out over the obstacle at **A**. Once your horse handles this easily, you can then place another 2-foot obstacle at the other end of the water jump, shown as **B** in the diagram. It is difficult for me to specify an exact distance from the bank into water to the next obstacle without seeing the actual water jump. Generally, you should place the obstacle at **B** on a series of strides from the water that will produce a comfortable, if not slightly forward, striding for your horse. As he gains confidence, you can move the obstacle at **B** closer to the water until he is jumping **A**, landing, taking a stride, jumping down into the water, cantering through the water, jumping from water to dry land, and then out over an obstacle at **B**.

The same comments apply now to the water as to the bank-and-ditch exercises: You can develop a wide range of variations on this basic theme. You can place obstacles in the water so that your horse must jump from the water and land back in the water. (Your long-suffering ground person will need a pair of rubber boots for this exercise.) You can create bounces, narrow fences, corners and turning questions, depending on the nature of the problem that you want your horse to learn to solve.

If you are going to go eventing or foxhunting with your horse, it is a good idea to travel your countryside and see what kind of problems you will encounter—not just at water complexes but at ditches, banks and so on. You can then come home and develop your own gymnastics to teach your horse to handle those problems easily and confidently.

Gymnastic 19 (p. 85)

In my opinion, cross country course designers these days are overusing the question of narrows and corners and ignoring the infinite possibilities of terrain. However, your training must prepare your horse for these questions, because it is almost a certainty that you will meet one of these obstacles at your next event.

Although narrow jumps are not exactly gymnastic fences as we have been describing them, narrows are such a useful exercise that I have included a section here on their presentation and training. By narrow jumps I also mean corners, chevrons, wedges and any obstacle where precision of presentation is required. As a general rule, I teach horses to approach gradually more and more narrow openings first, until they jump confidently through quite narrow openings. Typically, I ask my Novice- and Training-level horses to jump openings as narrow as 6 feet. At Preliminary and above, I make the openings 4-foot-6. I next teach them to jump a single fence on an angle, followed by multiple jumps on opposing angles, as shown on page 86. Once they master this, I feel they are ready for corners.

We will begin with narrow obstacles. To continue your horse's education in jumping on a straight line, use a 12-foot rail to build a 2-foot (60cm) vertical fence on the centerline of the arena and take an extra pair of post standards, placing them one on either side of the rail as shown in the upper left photo on page 89. Alternate the side the extra standards are on, so that the rail can be knocked down from either direction. The opening between the extra standards should be 10 feet (3m) at first, measured from their inside surfaces. Gradually decrease the opening until it is only 6 feet (1.5m) wide. Horses seem to understand this quite easily, and you will be surprised at the progress you can make and at how narrow an opening your horse will willingly jump through. Make sure you are able to canter over this narrow obstacle from both leads in both directions.

Once your horse jumps a narrow opening, you can build in-and-outs and gymnastics on related distances using extra standards to produce a narrower and narrower opening for him to negotiate.

The next step is to take rails that are approximately 6 feet (1.8m) long and build a 2-foot (60cm) vertical. Put a wing on either side of the narrow jump, which will frame the fence in an attractive manner for your horse, as shown

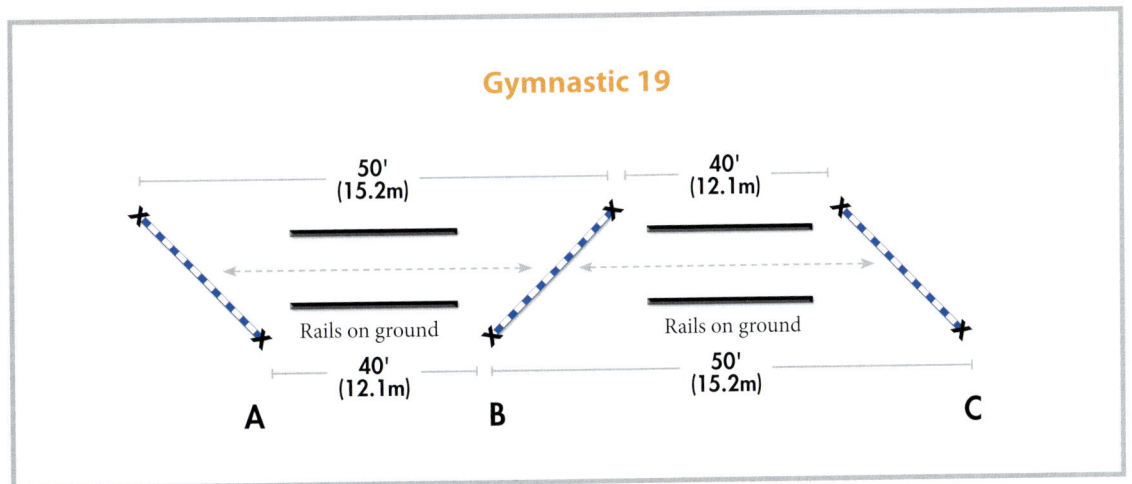

Gymnastic 19

GYMNASTIC 19A Straightness is a sign of balance. Gymnastic 19 will help you train your horse to jump straight through a series of obstacles. It is difficult to see from this perspective, but note that the verticals in these photos are not parallel; they are set at angles to each other. Alyssa Peterson and Two Rivers Run have practiced over two verticals in a row, with ground poles between them to guide "Ziggy," and I have just added a third vertical and two additional ground poles. If you look closely at Ziggy's right knee, you can see why I wanted him to practice this particular gymnastic. Usually, when a horse is low with one knee, he is on his forehand to that side. Before Alyssa headed towards this gymnastic, I told her, "I want you to think to yourself that your line is straight; it's the jumps that are crooked. Keep your right leg on at the girth, and soften your left leg."

Horses that approach an obstacle straight but land at an angle are pushing more with one hind leg than the other. Use the same aids you would if your horse were lazy with one hind leg during his dressage work: Close your leg at the girth. Always straighten him with your legs, not your reins. You can see that Alyssa has taken my comment about her leg aids seriously, and her legs are correct for a horse that is heavy on his right shoulder at the point of takeoff. Except for the uneven front end, so far, so good.

in the upper right photo on page 89. Trot and canter back and forth until he is relaxed jumping over the narrow obstacle. Later, you can raise the obstacle to increase the difficulty. I like for horses to be able to jump 3 inches higher than the requirements for their competitive level, i.e. 3-foot-6 for Training level.

Once you feel confident about this, you can remove the wings from the narrow jump, as shown in the lower left photo on page 89. However, you should lower the rails 6 inches until you are sure your horse is trustworthy. If he starts to swerve to one side or the other, you are better off replacing the wings until he willingly remains straight in the approach and the departure.

Now we will take the straightness concept another step. To build Gymnastic 19, first place six standards as shown on page 85. This will help you build the "to-and-fro rails," so-called because each rail is at an angle to the next. I use this exercise for several reasons: It teaches horses and riders to jump angled fences, it teaches horses and riders to prevent "drifting" in one direction or another while jumping angled fences, and it is an excellent preparation for jumping corner fences. Once you have the standards placed and mea-

Cross-Country Gymnastics

⬆ **GYMNASTIC 19B** Alyssa has done a good job with Ziggy up to this point. She is straight, poised over his center of gravity and looking ahead. Although her leg aids are still correct, we can see trouble brewing when we look at Ziggy's right knee. It is even lower than in the first photo, meaning that his loss of balance over his right shoulder is becoming more pronounced.

⬆ **GYMNASTIC 19C** Uh-oh. Now you can see why this is a good exercise for Ziggy. Although Alyssa has maintained her right leg against the girth, Ziggy is taking advantage of the fact that there is no guide pole after the third vertical and is drifting badly to his right. His low right knee would produce a dangerous situation if these were solid obstacles.

Obviously, Ziggy will practice this gymnastic until his balance improves enough that he jumps with his knees square and lands after the last obstacle still on a straight line. In addition, during his dressage work we will emphasize turn on the forehand to the left, right leg-yielding, right shoulder-in and turn on the haunches to the right. In other words, we will practice dressage exercises that improve Ziggy's sensitivity to Alyssa's right leg.

sured, using 12-foot rails, build a 2-foot vertical at **A**. Trot back and forth over this in both directions, passing through the other open standards. Then canter back and forth quietly, again passing through the open standards.

Once your horse is quiet and confident, place two poles on the ground about 10 feet (3m) apart between **A** and **B**, as shown. Make sure these poles are aligned correctly; this will help you stay straight as this exercise develops. Note the dotted line in the diagram of Gymnastic 19 (page 85). In order to help riders visualize this dotted line while they are practicing the exercise, I have the ground crew put a small pile of footing exactly in the middle of each rail. I want you to look at the jump anyway, and this reinforces the technique. While riding through the exercise, your attitude should be that your alignment is straight while the jumps are crooked.

Approach at the trot from the open standards at **C** and **B**, trot through the poles on the ground and jump the vertical at **A**. If your horse is not claustrophobic going through the ground poles from **B** to **A**, trot back the other direction. If your horse is reluctant, make the opening between the ground poles larger until he regains his confidence; some horses are claustrophobic about landing into narrow openings. After a few repetitions at the trot, your horse should be ready to add a 2-foot vertical at **B**.

It is in the nature of gymnastic work that we gradually increase the number of obstacles the horse must confront. When dealing with symmetrical gymnastics, horses should approach from the new end first. Green horses tend to focus on any change in their environment. Because of this, you should approach the new vertical from **B** to **A**. The distance between **B** and **A** should produce three relaxed strides from the trot, and later on three slightly quiet strides at the canter. The first time you trot the new vertical, your horse may be a little sticky and slow off the ground. However, as he lands behind **B** he will realize that he has already successfully dealt with the rest of the gymnastic and will usually jump out confidently. Repeat **B** to **A** until he is calm and balanced at the trot or the canter.

Place the next set of ground poles between **B** and **C** as shown, the same width apart as the poles between **A** and **B**. Trot through the new ground poles to jump **B** and **A** as before, reverse, jump from **A** to **B** at the trot, and then canter the exercise from both directions. Once you construct the vertical at **C**, your horse is now ready to trot the complete gymnastic. As before, approach from **C** first, before jumping from **A**. The vertical at **C** is the new element, and your horse will focus on it until he understands the nature of the question. Hopefully, he is now equally calm and balanced at either trot or canter, and from either direction.

The next step is to remove the ground poles between **A** and **B** and between **B** and **C**. Take the vertical at **C** down, but keep it handy … we will put it back in a moment. Canter back and forth from **A** to **B** and from **B** to **A** a couple of times. Now the fun begins. Most horses drift (veer slightly left or right in the approach and landing), and cantering this exercise without the ground poles will quickly demonstrate your horse's weak side. The typical experience is that while you were using the ground poles, you felt that three quiet strides was not short or long, but just natural. However, without the ground poles you feel quite comfortable taking three strides between **A** and **B**, but feel that the distance is a bit short

Introducing Narrows and Low-Wide Oxers

⬆ Using two extra standards, you can imitate a narrow jump of any height and width, as described on page 85. The two extra standards are placed on opposite sides of the vertical for safety reasons. The narrow vertical shown here is too high and too narrow for introductory work. If your horse has never done a narrow fence, open the extra standards as much as possible and put the vertical rail on the ground between the jump standards. Walk your horse back and forth over the rail on the ground. He will soon get the idea, and you can gradually raise the vertical and close the opening.

⬆ Once your horse understands narrow openings, you can introduce him to typical narrow rails and planks like this one. However, use wings at first. Keep the narrow obstacle small enough that you can worry about your rhythm rather than your timing.

⬆ Later on, discard the wings. I want you to be able to canter quietly back and forth over any sort of narrow obstacle you will meet in competition. Don't wait for the competition to introduce your horse to something new.

⬆ This is what I refer to as a "low-wide" oxer. During my gymnastic work, I will make these low-wide oxers much wider than they are high, which will cause your horse to stretch his body. At the same time, the diagonal rail on top of the oxer prevents your horse from thinking the oxer has become a bounce.

when jumping from **B** to **A**. The explanation is that your horse is drifting to the left; you will have slightly more room between **A** and **B** when you drift left, but slightly less room jumping from **B** to **A**. Before you start pulling on the right rein trying to straighten your horse, however, let's think the problem through.

A horse drifts because he is pushing with one hind leg more than the other. This can happen either in the approach or at the moment of takeoff. Your actions should be the same in both cases: Take away the leg that might be causing your horse to drift and try again. If your horse is drifting to the left, soften your right leg as you approach and jump **A** and **B**. In many cases, this is sufficient to straighten him. I believe riders should always think their problems through by asking themselves what it is they might be doing that would cause their horses to misbehave. This is a good guideline for most situations. For example, if your horse is rushing, don't kick him. If your horse is sluggish off the ground, make sure your hands are soft and quiet. If your horse is veering to the left, don't touch him with your right leg. While simplistic, this kind of change is often sufficient to correct your problem. If not, at least you know you can be part of the solution. By this I mean if you soften your right leg and your horse still drifts left, you can now add another aid—in this case, you should increase the pressure of your left leg at the girth. If he still drifts, keep your leg at the girth and add

> *It is a common mistake to relax your corrective aids after you are successful at the first obstacle; suddenly you will find your horse is drifting again, with predictably uncomfortable results.*

a left neck rein and a right opening rein. Make sure you move both hands equally if you need to resort to these aids. It is a common mistake to open the rein too much without supporting that aid with the leg and bearing-rein aids on the other side. This sequence of corrective aids is very important for eventing riders to understand, because so many current cross-country questions are questions involving accuracy of alignment.

Returning to Gymnastic 19, once you can keep your horse straight between **A** and **B** or **B** and **A**, it is time to replace the rail at **C**. If you were able to keep your horse straight between two obstacles, you should be able to keep him straight between three, as long as you maintain your corrective aids through the entire exercise. (It is a common mistake to relax your corrective aids after you are successful at the first obstacle; suddenly you will find your horse is drifting again, with predictably uncomfortable results.) Eventually your horse should be able to successfully jump the to-and-fro rails from both directions with the rails set at the height of your horse's competitive level; i.e. 3-foot-6 for Preliminary.

Before we take up the subject of corners, I want you to take another look at the diagram of Gymnastic 19 on page 85. Imagine what would happen if you extended the line formed by **A** and **B** downward, mentally ignoring **C**. At some point, you would create an exercise that required two strides; extending the lines farther would create a one-stride distance. Although I disapprove of angled bounces, due to the danger of a horse hitting an angled rail with one knee on the way up, one could conceivably draw the converging lines close enough together to form such a question. If we continue to extend them, as the lines intersect they will form a corner. In effect, while you were practicing Gymnastic 19, you were also rehearsing the skills you will need to jump a corner. By jumping the rail at **A**, you are also jumping the front rail of a corner, and at **B** you are jumping the back rail of a corner. Once you have become proficient at this exercise, it is time to introduce you and your horse to corners.

Corners consistently produce problems. When you look at a corner, the problem is obvious: The narrow point at one side of the obstacle invites your horse to refuse. Still, even when a problem is obvious, it is still a problem, and we need to be ready to deal with it.

Fortunately, you have already practiced the skills you will need to jump corners successfully. The vast majority of problems at corners occur because the horse ducks past the point of the corner at the last moment. In my opinion, this happens because riders "ride from their eyes, not their legs." By this I mean that riders have a subconscious tendency to relax their aids when their strides to the jump become predictable. Three strides away from a corner, it is not enough for the riders to see their strides—they must remember to tell their horses. Thanks to Gymnastic 19, you know how to keep your horse straight with one leg at the girth; now, just remember to keep your horse straight at the instant of takeoff. However, it might be better if we used the term "alignment" rather than "straight" when discussing corners, because we do not really approach corners the same way we were taught to approach normal obstacles.

Corners are easy to jump if you are accurate in your alignment. You cannot jump corners successfully by approaching perpendicular to the front rail; that increases the spread to a dramatic degree. Nor can you approach perpendicular to the back rail; that invites your horse to run out toward the single post standard. Instead, imagine a third rail—higher than the two rails forming the corner—bisecting the angle of the corner. You then approach on a line that is perpendicular to that imaginary rail. This allows you to ride on a straight line over the corner.

If the corner is, for example, a left point (which means that the two rails of the corner come together at the left side of the fence as you approach), I tell riders that if they are going to make a mistake in their alignment, in this instance they should ride a tiny bit from left to right. The advantage of this is that it gives the rider a split-second longer to correct the situation, should her horse lose confidence and attempt to duck out. Making the opposite mistake—aligning from right to left—increases the chances that the horse will refuse.

Introduce your horse to corners by building a corner using three standards and two rails. For purposes of discussion, I will describe a left-point corner, one that during competition would have a white flag on the point. Use two cups on the single standard, and remember to always put the front rail of the corner in a cup that is 3-6 inches lower, so as to produce a round face to the obstacle. At first, the spread between the pair of standards should be 3 feet or less. Set the back rail at about 2 feet, put the front rail in the lower cup of the single standard, and place the other end on the ground so that it is merely an attractive ground line for a 2-foot vertical fence. Canter over this obstacle a few times, perpendicular to the back rail the first time, and then at a slight right-to-left angle, to mentally prepare you and your horse for the next level of difficulty.

If your horse maintains his rhythm, you can now raise the front rail up into the cups—always making sure that the back rail of the corner is slightly higher than the front rail, just as you would with a round oxer. Once your horse is confident jumping a left-point corner, reverse the two rails on the single standard. This now creates a right-point, or red flag, corner. Again, canter over the right-point corner until you and your horse are equally confident over either left-point or right-point corners. If you have trouble visualizing your alignment, have the ground person momentarily rest an extra rail at the intersection of the two rails of the corner while you stand in front of the corner. Make sure the temporary rail exactly bisects the angle formed by the two rails forming a corner, then visualize a perpendicular approach to that temporary rail. Once you have done this, you can have your ground person take the rail away and approach with that alignment at the canter. If you still have trouble visualizing your approach, place two small piles of footing on the top of the two rails, in similar fashion to the suggestion in Gymnastic 19. Make sure the two visual aids are at the correct alignment.

Just as with Gymnastic 19, I eventually want you to be able to jump a corner that is set at the height of your competitive level. While you should be conservative about the spread of the corner, later on you can increase this spread to 9 feet (2.7m). This will truly give you and your horse the sensation of jumping a corner.

Once your horse is consistently jumping corners well, you should begin to jump them in combinations. When building corner combinations, be careful with the alignment of the two corners; your intention is to promote a straight line over the narrower parts of the corners, an area I sometimes refer to as "jumping the inner third of the corner." Jump the combination with 24 feet (7.3m), 36 feet (11m) or 48 feet (14.6m) measured from point to point, with both corners pointing the same way at first. Later on build a combination with the corners opposed; for example, a left-point corner followed by a right-point corner. These combinations are difficult to construct, and you must be very exact about the alignment of the two corners. Opposed corners are a serious test of straightness and are not suitable at or below the Preliminary level. At the upper levels of eventing, if you can jump opposed corners 36 feet (11m) apart, set at 3-foot-6 or higher, with the outside standards spread to a minimum of 9 feet, you can be well pleased with your state of training.

7
Exercises for Correcting Errors

It is inevitable in the training of any horse that problems in specific areas will develop. If your horse continually makes an error, you need to analyze what he is doing wrong and set up exercises to teach him what you want him to do.

Running Out

Refusals or "run-outs" are some of the most common jumping mistakes you will encounter during your horse's training.

If your horse continually runs out (for example) to the left, the simplest means of correction is to put an additional rail on top of the standard. Do not put this rail in a cup, because if your horse jumps off to the side badly and hits the wing, resting it in a cup has the effect of making the rail into a solid obstacle. If the rail is on top of the post, it will be easily dislodged.

Of course, if your horses drifts this extremely, you should increase and improve his dressage work. This will refine his sensitivity to your aids on the side on which he tends to run out. In addition, horses of this nature benefit from work over narrow fences and corners such as those described at the end of Chapter 6.

Drifting

A horse that jumps but swerves across the fence, landing on a different line from the one on which he took off, is said to be "drifting." Your horse does this because he is pushing more with one hind leg than the other and landing with the weight more on one shoulder than the other.

As with most jumping problems, work on the flat is the first place to start. If your horse jumps to the left, you should emphasize left leg-yielding, left shoulder-in and right turn on the haunches in order to put his body more into alignment.

When your horse drifts, one of the simplest and most effective means of straightening him is to apply one leg at the girth at the moment of takeoff. Notice that I said "leg" and not "legs." Your horse is pushing more with one hind leg than the other, and you should close your leg on the lazy side. If he jumps to the left, close your left leg, and vice versa. With extremely sensitive horses, make sure you soften the leg on the opposite side as well. Many times, just releasing the pressure on that side will be sufficient to straighten a sensitive horse.

Another way to straighten horses that drift while jumping is to put a half crossrail up behind a normal vertical. Place the half crossrail behind the vertical; allow a space the width of the rail between the obstacle and the half crossrail so that if your horse hits the vertical rail, there is room for it to fall out of the cup. (Do not place the half crossrail in a cup at the top of the standard; this causes the fence to be fixed, and you want the rail to fall away if your horse makes a mistake.)

Other means of correcting a horse that drifts:

- Place rails on the ground perpendicular to the fence in front of and after a fence, on the side towards which your horse drifts. Start with the ground poles perpendicular to the end of the fence, and then roll them more into your horse's path until you achieve the desired effect. This will help some horses, although I have not found it to be as efficient as the leg at the girth or the half crossrail.

- Jump a small obstacle on a circle in the opposite direction to your horse's drift. For example, if he continually lands to the left, circle to the right after landing. Basically, you are going to teach your horse to jump in the opposite direction from the direction of his drift.

Rushing

"Rushing," or suddenly accelerating in the approach to an obstacle, is the most common flaw in the horse's training. You need a wide range of techniques to deal with this problem. If your horse starts to rush, we can go back to Gymnastic 5 on page 34, which is an excellent exercise to teach your horse to remain rhythmical in the approach to the obstacle. The double bounce at the end of the line of obstacles used in this gymnastic has the effect of training your horse not to overcommit himself, and teaches him to compress his body after several jumping efforts. If your horse is beginning to rush, first revisit Gymnastic 5 and see if that helps. However, not every horse will react favorably to Gymnastic 5; you may need other tools to explain to your horse what you want from him.

Gymnastic 20 (p. 96)

This exercise, which is quite simple, will also serve to calm a rushing horse. As shown on page 96, build eight small obstacles at the corners, approximately 2 feet high to start. (You can raise them once you know your horse understands the question.) This will have the effect of forming an 80-foot (24.3m) square box that is open on the sides.

Warm your horse up over a few individual fences elsewhere in the arena and then canter him on a circle inside the box. This circle will give you a choice of four fences that you can jump on either lead. Do not jump any of them until your horse is settled on the circle, then leave the circle and jump a fence. At first you can land on the lead of your horse's choosing, but later you should begin to select the lead on which he will land. To do this, review the aids you used in Gymnastic 8, page 50, when you first taught your horse to change leads and direction over a fence.

Landing after a fence with a horse that is rushing will usually be a fairly enthusiastic production; immediately turn back into the box and resume the circle. It may take several revolutions before your horse settles, but do not jump again until you have re-established his calmness. You can increase the difficulty of this exercise by jumping into the box over one of the corner obstacles and cantering

GYMNASTIC 20A Gymnastic 20 is a good training technique if your horse wants to speed up at his jumps. Claire Kelley and Orion XII are cantering inside the four-cornered arena formed by the rails and standards, as shown in the graphic on page 96. Orion is obviously thinking about the vertical that is just out of our view. Claire is in lovely balance here, with soft hands and a quiet lower leg. She will go as deep into the corner as she can without provoking Orion, but he does not get to jump—yet.

GYMNASTIC 20B We cannot see his face from our vantage point, but I can guarantee you that Orion is eyeing the next vertical hopefully and gathering himself to jump the next obstacle that has come into view. Again, Claire will ride as deeply into the corner as Orion's nerves will allow.

GYMNASTIC 20C Not yet, Orion. At the last possible second, Claire has opened her inside rein and closed her outside leg to turn Orion along the next side of the enclosure.

GYMNASTIC 20D At last, Orion gets his reward for being good. After jumping out of the enclosure, Claire has the option of circling at the far end of the arena and then jumping back in, or she can circle at the end of the arena and then enter the enclosure across the diagonal, change leads and repeat this gymnastic on the right lead. The key to using this gymnastic is that your horse must be calm and balanced before he is rewarded with another jump.

around the circle until your horse is calm and balanced again.

Work in both directions until you have jumped all eight fences from the canter. This exercise takes some time to complete, but it is effective as long as you are dedicated to re-establishing your horse's balance and mental discipline after each fence before continuing to the next jump.

Popping the Shoulder

Another common bad habit is for horses to "pop" their shoulders when going around a course, meaning that they turn their heads to the outside of a turn and put their weight over their inside shoulders. Horses that take this shape rarely ar-

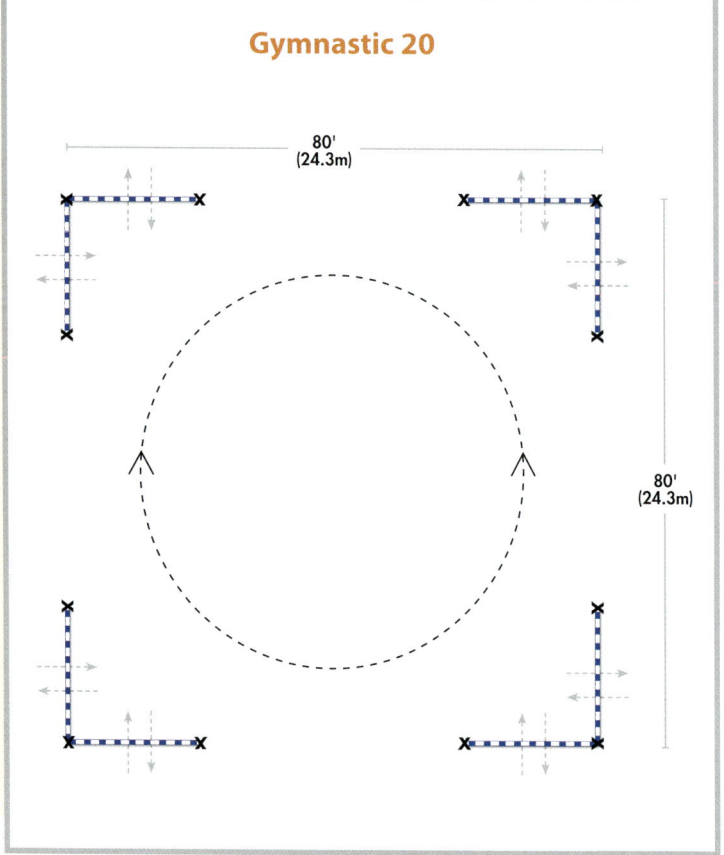

rive at an obstacle in balance. The purpose of the next gymnastic is to teach your horse not to pop his shoulder while going through a turn, which will make him more rideable around a course.

Gymnastic 21 (below)

For this gymnastic, you will need two verticals and two oxers placed as shown in the diagram. If at all possible, it is best to try this gymnastic in an indoor arena or an outdoor arena with a substantial fence around the perimeter. The arena wall or the perimeter fence has a powerful effect on horses that want to rush. To execute the turns, you should use the same aids as you did during Gymnastics 8 and 9 (pages 50 and 54).

As usual, start with the obstacles about 2 feet high with the oxers at no more than a 2-foot-6 spread. The distances specified should be measured from the arena wall or perimeter fence. If you do not have an enclosed area, you can put extra standards at the measured distances to give you a reference as to the size and shape of the curves that you will describe while doing this gymnastic. However, the exercise will work best in an indoor school or a well-fenced area.

Start with a 2-foot vertical placed at **A**, as shown in the diagram. Canter on the left hand through the open standards at **B**, jumping **A**. Turn left into the arena wall, re-establish the left canter lead, continue left down the long side and then again turn left through the open standards at **B** and jump **A**, again turning left. You should continue this until your horse anticipates the left turn back into the corner and lands in balance. Use the aids we discussed in Gymnastics 8 and 9 to teach your horse to land on the lead you select.

After your horse is comfortable with the approach and the turn on the left lead, move to the other side of the arena and do the same thing on the right lead. Canter on the right lead through the open standards at **D**, jumping the small vertical at **C** and turning to the right through the corner. Continue down the long side, turn back to the right through the open standards at **D**, and so on. Just as with the first obstacle on the left lead, you should continue this until your horse begins

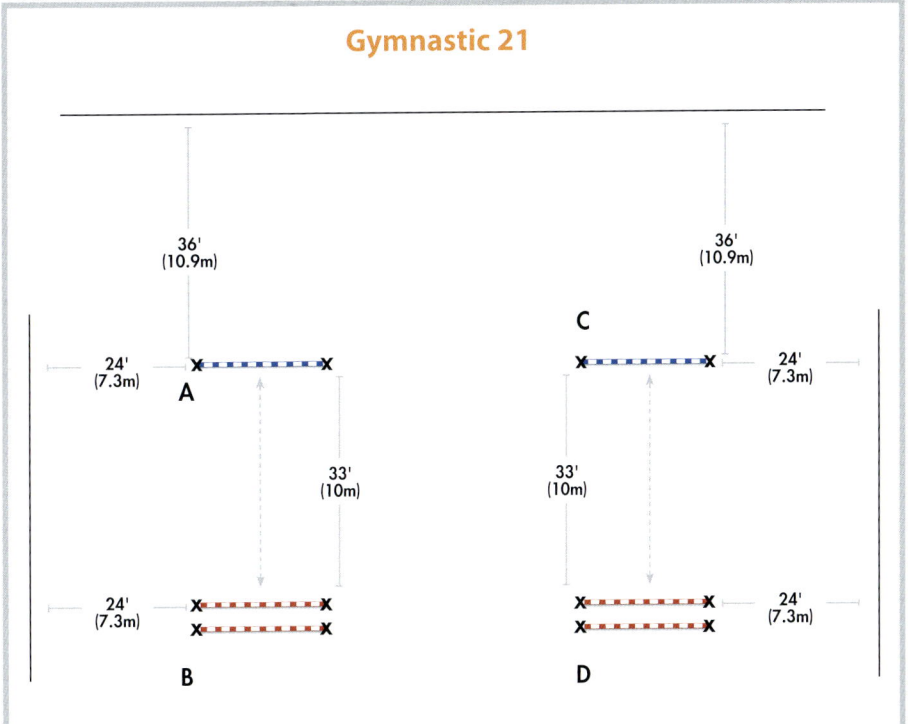

to anticipate turning back into the wall and lands on the right lead.

It should now be possible for you to start out on the left lead down the long side, turning back towards **A**, jumping and landing on the left lead. Continue on the left lead and turn across the arena through the open standards at **D** and jump the small obstacle at **C**, landing on the right lead. You can now repeat this figure-eight pattern beginning on the right lead. Repeat this variation of a "figure-eight" exercise several times and then walk.

While you and your horse catch your breath, have your ground person build small oxers at **B** and **D**, approximately 2 feet high and 2-foot-6 wide. Repeat the exercise as before, beginning on the left lead, turning back, jumping the oxer at **B**, taking two quiet strides, jumping the vertical at **A** and

⬆ GYMNASTIC 21A Gymnastic 21 makes your horse easier to ride over stadium courses at a competition. When he gets to the end of the arena, he soon learns he is going to turn to the inside. It is not long, however, before he is dropping his inside shoulder and cutting across the arena on his forehand, a habit that will cause problems as you approach another obstacle after your turn out of the short end of the arena.

Gymnastic 21 is really two identical gymnastics placed close to the end of the arena, and needs an enclosed area to produce the desired result.

The placement of these two gymnastics makes it possible for you to turn either direction from either gymnastic. Once you have turned both ways out of the gymnastic, your horse can no longer predict which direction you will turn, and he will learn to wait for you.

Skyeler Icke Voss and Accolade have approached in the canter, and are landing behind the small oxer in the background. This oxer corresponds to D in the graphic on page 97. At this point, you cannot guess which way Skyeler is going to turn. The distance between the oxer and the vertical at C allows for two strides. As your horse steps onto his takeoff point in front of the vertical at C, you should ask him to land on the right lead. (Use the skills you learned during Gymnastic 8, where you practiced landing on alternate leads.)

Skyeler knows which way she is going to turn, but "Cody" does not, which causes him to wait for instructions.

turning left. Repeat this several times, then take another break.

Resume work, this time on the right lead, and jump from **D** to **C** in two strides, turning right after **C** and so on. Again, after several repetitions, take a break.

Later, you can vary this exercise slightly. For example, on the right lead you can approach

⬆ **GYMNASTIC 21C** There is enough room in this gymnastic to be able to turn right, but only enough, and Skyeler is still gauging her turn, making sure that Cody stays on the path she has selected for him. Cody looks slightly on his forehand in the turn, and Skyeler should engage her inside leg through the corner. Cody has had enough dressage training to be able to go through the corner in shoulder-in. This will help teach him to remain in self-carriage going through his turns. Make sure you practice this gymnastic on both sides of the arena. Your horse will find one direction easier than the other, which is valuable information. If Cody finds turning to the right more difficult, we will emphasize that direction and increase his lateral work on that side to develop the engagement of his inside leg. Many of our jumping problems can be cured by our dressage work.

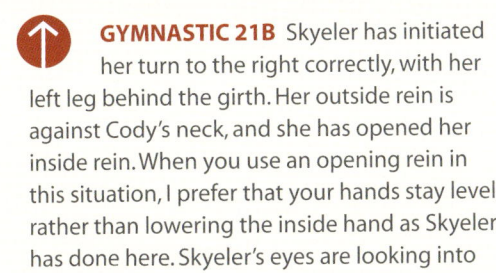

⬆ **GYMNASTIC 21B** Skyeler has initiated her turn to the right correctly, with her left leg behind the girth. Her outside rein is against Cody's neck, and she has opened her inside rein. When you use an opening rein in this situation, I prefer that your hands stay level, rather than lowering the inside hand as Skyeler has done here. Skyeler's eyes are looking into her turn, and Cody is responding correctly.

from the wall towards **A**, landing on the left lead, turning back into the wall and approaching on an angle to **B**. After **B**, turn back to the right on the right lead and jump **A** on an angle again and so on.

After your horse figures this out, take another break and do the same "figure-eight" exercise between **C** and **D**. Begin on the left lead, approaching from between the wall and the oxer at **D**, and jump the small vertical at **C**. Land on the right lead turning out of the corner to approach the oxer at **D** on a slight left angle, land after **D** and turn back to **C**, and so on.

Changing Leads

When doing a course of show jumps, it is a great advantage to be able to select the lead that you want before you approach the next obstacle. The following exercise is designed to help you teach your horse to land on a lead that you have selected. Note that you should also be practicing flying changes with your horse. While flying changes are dressage movements and this book is confined to gymnastic exercises, you should teach a young horse flying changes soon after he is confirmed in his canter lead departures. (Remember that young horses should be asked for flying changes from a natural frame, not a compressed frame.) If your horse knows how to land on the lead that you select over an obstacle *and* how to do a flying change, you now have two chances of approaching the next obstacle on the course with the correct (inside) lead.

Gymnastic 22 (below)

Sometimes the simplest gymnastics are the best. Build four jumps on the centerline of your arena, as shown. I typically start the obstacles at 2 feet, with a ground line on each side. You can raise them later, as appropriate. **A** and **B**, and **C** and **D,** should be at right angles to each other. Have at least 45 feet (22.8m) between the corners at which the two fences join, and place a single post standard at least 60 feet (25.9m) away from the inside of the corner where **A** meets **B**.

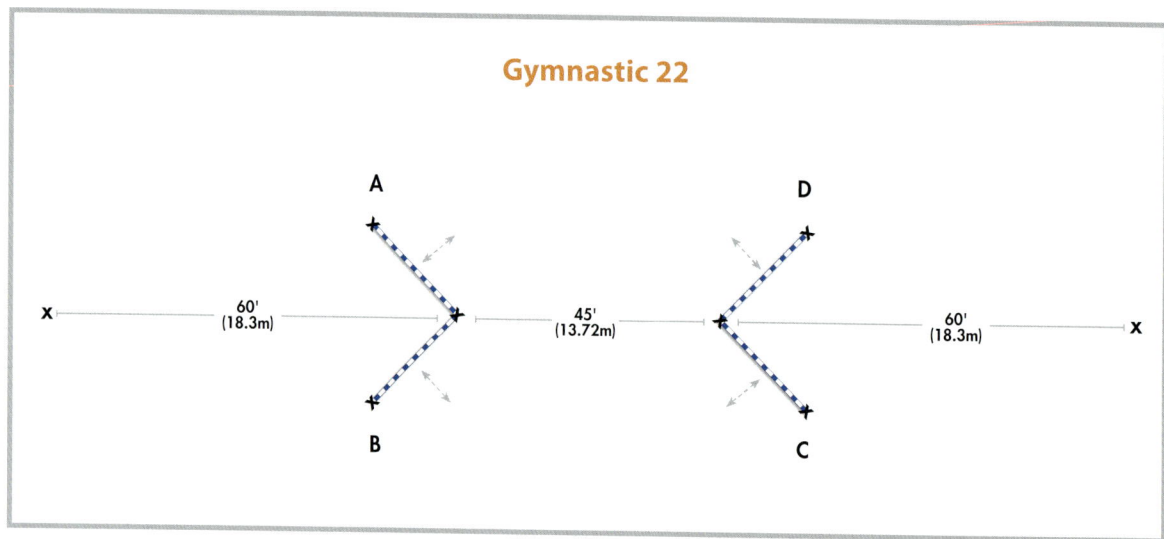

100 MODERN GYMNASTICS

Exercises for Correcting Errors

GYMNASTIC 22 is difficult to visualize. If you look at the graphic on page 100, we are standing below A and B. Think of a figure eight, starting on the right lead around the plain standard closest to us. That is where Tracey Cover and Vienna start; they are now in the approach to the closest vertical on the right of the standard. Using the skills they learned in Gymnastic 8 (changes of direction), Tracey and Vienna will plan to approach on the right lead, jump the vertical at B, land on the left lead and proceed on a curve around the standard at the far end of the arena. These standards are used to help you make precise turns. Eventually, you should be able to do this gymnastic without the standards. The far standard is obscured in this image, but you can locate it in the graphic.

As Tracey makes her turn at the far end of the figure eight, she has several options. She can circle without jumping, if Vienna is too excited to jump well. She can make a short turn back to the C in your graphic, or, as she has done here, she can proceed on a large, gentle curve all the way back to the vertical at A. Given that Vienna has won working hunter classes at most of the major horse shows on the East Coast, we should not be surprised by the lovely shape that she takes over the vertical at A. The next time around the figure eight, Tracey makes a more difficult turn to jump C. She has taken care of business, and in the farthest image you can see that Vienna is landing on the right lead.

Regardless of your decision as you practice this gymnastic, the important things to remember are to maintain a very steady rhythm around the figure eight, and to make sure you land on the opposite lead each time you jump.

This exercise is a continuation of the skills you and your horse learned in Gymnastics 8 and 9, so I suggest you review that section before attempting this work. Start in canter over **A** on the left lead, making sure that you ask for the right lead at the moment of takeoff. When you land, continue past **D** and **C** on the right lead, turn back to your right and approach **B**. Make sure that you are perpendicular to **B** in the approach and that when you take off at **B** you ask for the left lead. Continue straight for a few strides on the left lead and then turn behind the post standard on the center line and re-approach **A** on the left lead. Continue along this "figure-eight" path for several repetitions; then walk, give your horse a break and resume work on the right lead.

Now your path will proceed as follows: Approaching **B** from beyond the post standard in a right lead canter, jump **B** and land on your left lead. Continue behind **C** and **D** on the left lead, controlling your curve until your approach is perpendicular to jump **A**. Land on the right lead, continue behind the post standard and resume the figure eight. Again you should stay on this figure eight until your horse is relaxed and changes leads over each jump. If you have trouble with this, you should attempt the "clover-leaf" pattern in Chapter 5, which is Gymnastic 8 on page 50, and practice the aids you need for changing lead over the obstacles. Gymnastic 8 is much easier than 22 because you do not need timing to execute the lead change; the set distances will tell you when to apply your aids.

Once your horse has obviously learned what we are trying to teach him, you can vary this basic pattern in several ways. For example, approach **A** on the left lead. This time, turn inside of **D** and **C** and continue on a curve back to **B**. Landing after **B**, turn back to the left inside the single post standard and continue on a curve back again to **A**. Remember to keep the curve at the top and bottom of the arena symmetrical, so that as you leave the turn, you are once again perpendicular to the next fence.

If your horse has mastered this exercise you can start to jump, for example, from **A** to **D** (for the first time in this gymnastic) back to **B** and then from **A** straight ahead, turning right back to **C** and continuing on a curve back to **B** and so on.

There are any number of possible permutations and combinations; the key aspect is that your horse should land on the lead you have selected after each jump at the same speed with which you approached it. Strive for a clock-like regularity in the approach, the takeoff, the landing, and the departure.

Horses Who Slow at the Moment of Takeoff

If your horse "stalls" or is sticky at the moment of takeoff, you should first of all view this as a dressage problem. Your horse should land going at the same speed at which he takes off. If he gradually slows while working through your gymnastic exercises, he is getting behind your leg. A sharp prod with a spur or a quick reminder with a stick directly behind your leg will usually solve the problem. When a horse is slow off the ground, the rider often makes the mistake of speeding up in the approach and trying to make the horse stand off the obstacle. This mistake by your horse is not a mistake of speed or accuracy; it is a mistake of loss of impulsion at the takeoff and should be corrected there, by the spur and the stick. Strive to approach, jump, land, and depart all at the same speed.

Gymnastic 23 (below)

When I refer to your horse being "forward," I mean that you can ask for a longer step or stride and get an instantaneous response. If you continue to have difficulty with stickiness, set up Gymnastic 23 as shown on this page and practice through it several times. First, trot your horse over the placing rail 9 feet (2.7m) away from a 2-foot vertical at **A** until you feel he is warmed up. Before starting the next sequence, it is important that you understand how to solve the slightly long distance you are about to teach your horse. When dealing with variations of your horse's stride, it is essential that you apply the correct aids as you land after the first obstacle. When they attempt a long two-stride distance, for instance, too many riders' aids sound like this: land-one-***TWO***-oops! The correct solution is to sound like this: land-***ONE***-two. Do not wait until you are at the next obstacle to change your horse's length of stride. If the distance is long, you must make the alteration in the first stride, not the last. (For a short distance, although the theory remains the same, your aids are reversed. Handle an extremely short two-stride by half-halting at the moment of landing. If you jump into a short distance normally and allow your horse to take his usual stride, chances are you will have a front knockdown on your way out.)

Next, build a 2-foot-high by 2-foot-6-wide oxer at **B** and trot through again, landing at the canter after **A** and taking two strides from **A** to **B**. This distance will be slightly forward and you will have to keep your legs on in order not to have your horse "chip in" a third stride. When your horse is landing and taking the correct number of strides to **B**, then build a triple bar 3 feet high and 4 feet wide at **C**, 42 feet (12.8m) away from **B** as shown.

This exercise will now produce a rhythm of trot in, jump the vertical, land and take two strides, jumping the oxer at **B**. Concentrate on landing at the canter behind **B** going forward. Press your horse forward for three strides and jump the triple bar at **C**. Remember to keep your

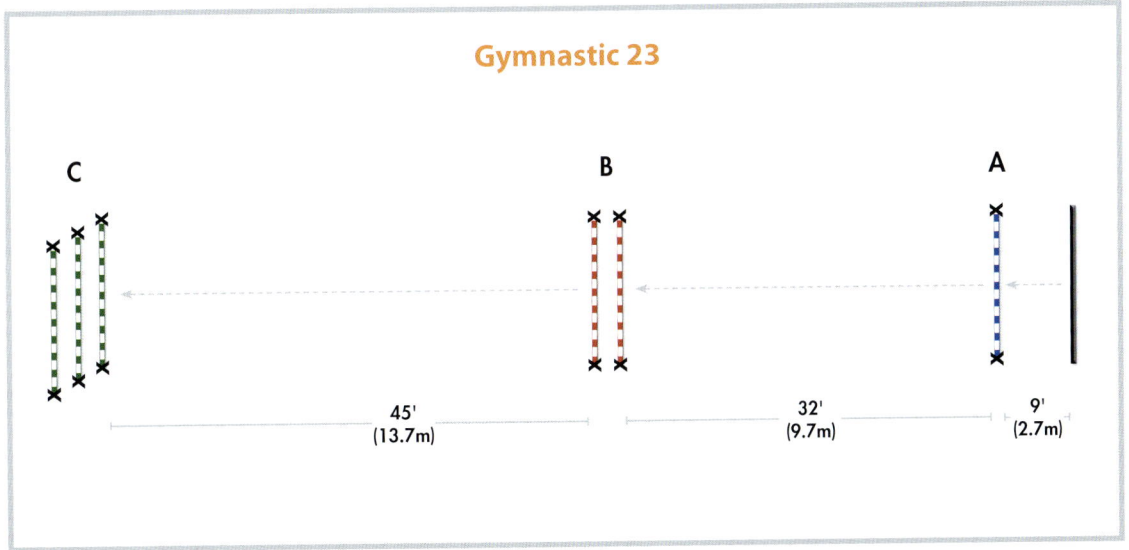

Gymnastic 23

GYMNASTIC 23A Gymnastic 23 does not suit every horse. If your horse has even the slightest tendency to speed up in his gymnastics or combinations, then 23 is not for him (and you). However, if he is sticky and lands in a heap on the other side of the fence, then 23 is part of the solution.

Skyeler Icke Voss and Accolade look great over the first vertical, although we can see that "Cody" has his left knee lower than his right. This is a sign that he is not symmetrical yet, and that we have to continue to train him to be equal on both reins. If your horse feels heavy to you on one side of his mouth, chances are he will hang a knee on that side over fences. The correction for this is more lateral work, teaching your horse to step from one leg to the opposite hand. That means Cody is going to do a great deal of left leg-yield and left shoulder-in, until he learns to keep equal weight in both shoulders as he jumps.

GYMNASTIC 23B The distance between the vertical and the first oxer (shown as **A** and **B** in the graphic on page 103) is long and the oxer is not huge—and Cody has not paid much attention to the oxer. His jumping technique over it looks rather casual, with his forearms barely at the horizontal and lower legs already opening up. This reaction is typical of horses that can jump a big fence; if they are not impressed, they will let you know. Skyeler, on the other hand, is quite impressed. She can see how big the triple bar ahead is and how much distance she and Cody have to cover, and she has lowered her seat closer to the saddle and is closing her legs. She will need to give a powerful aid to Cody, in order to motivate him to take long strides. If she can do this, they will step to the base of the triple-bar, which is the correct takeoff point for obstacles shaped like a staircase.

leg on at the point of takeoff over **C** so that your horse stretches out over the triple bar and lands at the same speed with which he took off.

Several repetitions of this exercise may be necessary in order to get your horse to begin to increase the length of his stride. As a general comment, do not ask him to lengthen for more than three strides at a time or you will find that he will begin to "sprawl" and go on his forehand.

Another exercise that may help keep your horse from "stalling" is to use ground lines both in front of and behind your obstacles. Make sure that the ground line in front of the obstacle is at least the height of the fence away from the fence, if not more, and certainly on the landing side the ground line

GYMNASTIC 23C Cody has responded very well, clearing this large triple bar by a huge margin. Because he respects this fence, he has used his hindquarters much better than he did over the previous oxer. Skyeler was worried about the long distance and the size of the triple bar, and she is still in a slightly defensive position, with her seat bones almost touching the saddle and Cody well out in front of her. Her lower leg is classically correct. Because of the security provided by a solid lower leg, she can apply her aids with cool precision. I especially like the soft feeling of her reins here. She is guiding but not interfering. Skyeler has allowed Cody to take her elbows forward, rather than bending over at the waist.

should be 6 inches to 1 foot (15-30cm) more than the height of the fence behind the obstacle. These rails will cause your horse to reach out more with his shoulders for the landing, thus taking a longer stride in the departure from the obstacle.

Knocking Fences Down In Front

Horses who hang their front legs are difficult to train to jump correctly. However, they can be improved. I personally do not "rap" or "pole" my horses, because event horses usually have to go across country before they show jump, and by the time you get to the show-jumping phase, your horse has forgotten all about his experiences of a week or so ago.

It is a common error for eventing horses, especially, to knock obstacles down in front. Many times this occurs because your horse has not learned to use his shoulders and hindquarters correctly. He has trouble "snapping" his knees because he is not active with his hindquarters. You must increase the swing of the hindquarters first, which will elevate the forehand, which will then cause the horse to become more efficient in his shoulders. The long distance between the obstacles in Gymnastic 23 will increase the activity of your horse's hindquarters, and the low-wide shape of the oxers will teach him to stretch and use his shoulders.

(Note the direct correlation between my comments here and classical dressage theory. Go forward first, then compress.)

I find that by jumping him over low-wide oxers and longer distances as shown in Gymnastics 6 and 23, I can teach the horse to draw his shoulder up and forward, which has the effect of teaching him how to use his shoulders correctly. I work over longer distances first and try to stretch the horse's shoulders out, and then I work him back into shorter and shorter distances with increasingly higher obstacles. The reason I do it this way is because I have found that if you compress the distance between obstacles first for a horse who is dangling his forehand, invariably you will cause him to jump higher but to dangle worse.

Knocking Down Fences Behind

Occasionally you will deal with horses that are a bit slow behind. Work this sort of horse through double-bounce oxers. Low oxers 3 feet (90cm) high and 3 feet (90cm) wide set 12 feet (3.6m) apart from the next oxer, and again 12 feet (3.6) apart from the next oxer, will many times cause the horse to follow through better with his hindquarters. Alternatively, rest two extra rails in an "A" shape over a 3-foot vertical and canter your horse over the point of the A. Usually he will bump the A once with his hind feet and then start to make a better effort. Rest the point of the A on the top of the vertical once, but then you will have to push the point 1 to 2 feet further beyond the top of the vertical to have an effect on your horse.

8
Conclusion

I hope that you have enjoyed this book and that your horse has improved his performance over jumps as a result of working through the gymnastics. A few principles are listed here to conclude this work and to provide you with a quick reminder in the future.

- Calm, forward and straight are all the rules for training horses you will ever need.

- When jumping, place your weight over your horse's shoulders and soften your reins. You will transform a dull slave into a joyful and willing partner.

- You will make better progress if you jump little and often.

- Keep the obstacles small until you are sure your horse understands the question you are asking. Once he understands, his God-given talent is the only real limit.

- Teach your horse new skills by breaking those skills down into their most basic components.

- Time spent on improving your own jumping position is never wasted. There is a strong relationship between how you ride and how your horse goes. To improve your horse, improve yourself.

- Deal with your horse's mistakes as lack of knowledge, rather than willful disobedience. Determine which part of the question your horse does not understand, and develop a way to explain it to him. I am sure he will respond and improve.

- As you go along in riding, you will develop your own system of training horses. Keep in mind the preface to the *U.S. Army Manual of Equitation,* 1921 Edition, which says that any system of training that destroys the tranquility of horses is defective.

A close partnership with a horse is one of the greatest pleasures known to mankind. I hope this book helps you to attain that partnership.

Bibliography

I hope you are interested enough in improving your own horse's performance to read further. Certainly people cannot learn how to ride without ever reading a book on the subject. Your progress will be much faster and your eventual results will be much better, if you study the basics of your sport.

You will find here a list of books on jumping, in the order that they appear on my library shelf. They made a great deal of sense to me when I read them, so much so that I wrote a book on the topic myself, which I include here.

I am sure your riding will improve if you apply some of the lessons to be learned from these books.

The de Némethy Method, Bertalan de Némethy
    Doubleday 1988

Riding and Jumping, William Steinkraus
    Doubleday 1961

Reflections on Riding and Jumping, William Steinkraus
    Doubleday 1991

Riding and Schooling Horses, Col. Harry D. Chamberlin
    Derrydale 1934

Training Hunters, Jumpers and Hacks, Col. Harry D. Chamberlin
    Derrydale 1937

Training Showjumpers, Anthony Paalman
    J. A. Allen 1998

Hunter Seat Equitation, George H. Morris
    Doubleday 1971

Winning with Frank Chapot, Frank Chapot
    Breakthrough Publications 1992

Anne Kursinski's Riding and Jumping Clinic, Anne Kursinski
    Doubleday 1995/Trafalgar Square Books 2011

Jumping is Jumping, Jane Wallace
    Methuen 1994

Training the Three Day Event Horse and Rider, James C. Wofford
    Doubleday 1995

About the Author

JAMES C. (JIM) WOFFORD, 68, was born and raised on a horse farm in Milford, Kansas. He is a graduate of Culver Military Academy and the School of Business at the University of Colorado (B.S. Bus. Admin. '69). A three-time Olympian, Jim has spent his life with horses and is one of the best-known eventing trainers in the world today. A Hall of Fame member of both the United States Eventing Association and Culver Military Academy, he trains at his farm in Upperville, Virginia, and travels extensively, teaching and giving clinics.

Jim has had at least one student on every U.S. Olympic, World Championship, and Pan American Games team since 1978. All four members of the U.S. bronze medal team at the 2000 Sydney Olympics, as well as individual gold medal winner David O'Connor, were graduates of the Wofford program. In addition, three of the four members of the 2002 World Equestrian Games gold medal team were his former students. Kim Severson, the individual silver medal winner at the Athens Olympics, and Gina Miles, the individual silver medal winner at the Bejing Olympics, are also both graduates of the Wofford program.

Jim was named U.S. Olympic Committee Developmental Coach of the Year in both 1998 and 1999. He coached the Canadian Team for the 2002 World Championships, the 2003 Pan American Championships (where Canada won a team silver medal), and the 2004 Olympics in Athens. In 2007 Jim was named a Fellow of the U.S. Eventing Association Instructor Certification Program.

Widely sought after as a clinician and coach, Jim Wofford is equally well-known as an author. His first book, *Training the 3-Day Event Horse and Rider,* is now back in print after selling out the first print run; his second book, *Gymnastics: Systematic Training of the Jumping Horse,* is out of print. A sequel, *Modern Gymnastics,* became available in April 2013.

Jim shares a passion for fishing with his grandson Lewis Ince.

His next three books, *Take a Good Look Around, 101 Eventing Tips,* and *Cross Country with Jim Wofford* are both available. In addition, he writes a monthly column for *Practical Horseman,* the largest monthly periodical in the U.S. dedicated to English riding.

Jim was a successful competitor until his retirement in 1986. He rode on the 1968, 1972 and 1980 Olympic teams, winning two team silver medals and one individual silver medal. He also competed in the 1970 and 1978 World Championships, winning bronze individual and team medals. He won the U.S. National Championships five times, on five different horses, and won or placed at many competitions abroad between 1959 and 1986.

In addition to Jim's eventing achievements, he was an active competitor in steeplechase races, rode in numerous horse shows, and fox hunted for more than 30 years. Jim and his wife of more than 45 years, Gail W. Wofford, ex-MFH, live at their farm in Upperville, Virginia. They have two daughters, Mrs. Timothy L. (Hillary) Jones and Mrs. Charles K. (Jennifer) Ince, and four grandsons—James Walker Jones, Hudson Wofford Jones, Lewis Kitchell Ince and Theodore Brown Ince. The entire family still rides. However, when the boys can sneak away, they go fishing as well.

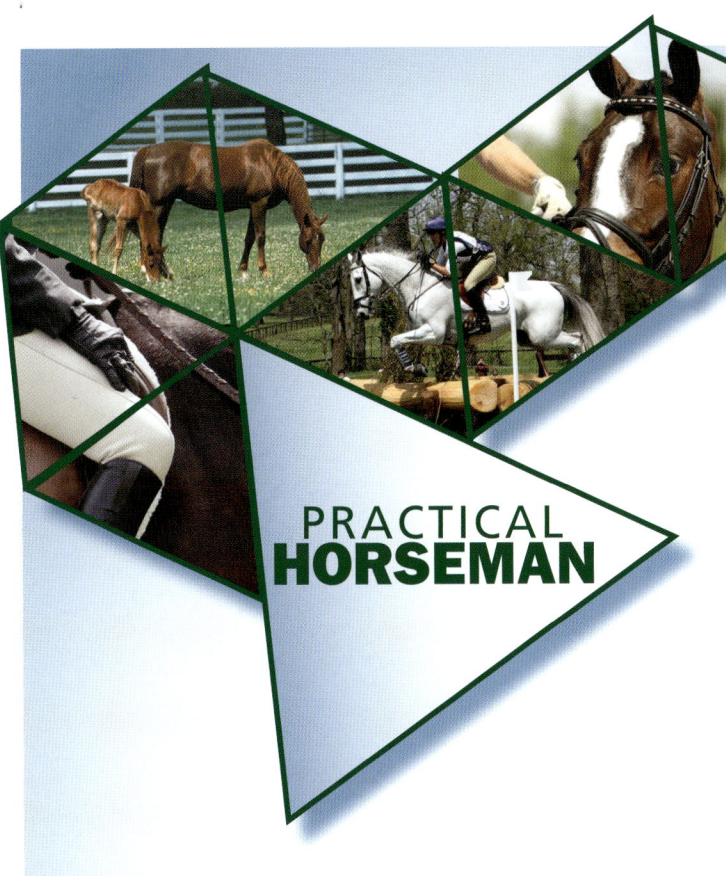

Expert How-To for English Riders

Practical Horseman is renowned for its award-winning step-by-step training articles, developed with leading riders and trainers to give both professional and amateur riders an edge. The pages of *Practical Horseman* will instruct, inform and inspire you issue after issue.

Subscribe today! Toll free 1-877-717-8929 or visit www.EquiSearch.com.

AIM EQUINE NETWORK
EQUUS – PRACTICAL HORSEMAN – HORSE & RIDER – DRESSAGE TODAY
AMERICAN COWBOY – SPIN TO WIN – TRAIL RIDER

www.EquiSearch.com – Equine.com – MyHorse.com – HorseBooksEtc.com